THIS IS ONLY A TEST

THIS IS ONLY A TEST

WHAT BREAST CANCER TAUGHT ME ABOUT FAITH, LOVE, HAIR, AND BUSINESS

CHRIS-TIA DONALDSON

MIRACLE PRESS

THIS IS ONLY A TEST
*What Breast Cancer Taught Me about
Faith, Love, Hair, and Business*

ISBN   978-1-5445-0304-2 *Hardcover*
       978-1-5445-0303-5 *Paperback*
       978-1-5445-0302-8 *Ebook*

To Mom, Dad, and the entire tgin team
for their never-ending support, constant encouragement,
and willingness to believe in my crazy ideas

CONTENTS

INTRODUCTION

I never set out to write a book about breast cancer. This time was one of the darkest periods in my life—one I didn't think I would have the strength to live through, one where I doubted my faith in God. As a result, I wanted to move on with my life after finishing treatment, but for one reason or another, people were able to relate to my story of overcoming adversity, even if they weren't personally dealing with this disease.

This book is as much for me as it is for you. The truth is I'm still scared—scared of dying, scared of my cancer coming back. But each and every day, as I wrestle with these thoughts, I commit to living, even though I know that we're all dying. There were so many things I chose to ignore and wipe away from my memory. Writing this book has allowed me, or perhaps forced me, to remember this painful time in my life and sit with my emotions rather than run from them.

My story is also meant to show you that your test—whether past, present, or future—is for a reason. It's an opportunity. It's preparing you for more and giving you a way to become more.

Throughout this book, I draw on my own personal experiences—building this company, dealing with relationships, and battling cancer—to give insight on how I found love, how I held onto faith through these challenging moments, and how I ultimately had to let go of my obsession with more achievement and success in order to be a better friend, daughter, businesswoman, and hopefully one day, wife and mother. I'm still a work in progress. In fact, I'm far from perfect. But what I am, is real.

I also hope that a little insight into my journey gives you that extra nudge you need when something doesn't feel right or when your girlfriend keeps ignoring whatever her body is trying to tell her. Please, listen to your body and trust what it is trying to tell you. And ladies, if you're over forty, please get your mammogram. If you're under forty and feel something strange in your breasts, talk to your doctor and insist on a mammogram, even if they tell you things are fine.

For those of you who are battling cancer or have a loved

one who has been diagnosed with this condition, I'm telling you my story to shed light on the emotions you, your mother, daughter, son, or best friend may be experiencing. In these situations, you have to decide whether you're going to accept your fate and let it take you into darkness, or whether you will fight and not allow your circumstances to define you.

Cancer is just one storm. It didn't define me, and you don't have to allow your storms to define you.

Finally, if you take anything from this book, take the opportunity to start putting yourself first. I offer my testimony, my path, as an intimate look into what living in a world where women don't take care of themselves looks like, particularly women of color, and how I opted to change my life as a result.

So, pull up a chair, pour yourself a nice, tall glass of wine, and get comfortable. Here we go. Raw, real stuff. My journey, as a gift to you: *This Is Only a Test: What Breast Cancer Taught Me about Faith, Love, Hair, and Business.*

Chapter One

THE BALI WITHIN

I was down to three pairs of clean underwear and two pairs of socks. For once in my life, I packed light. I had come to Bali almost three weeks ago with a pair of flip-flops, two bathing suits, twenty-one pairs of underwear, ten black Old Navy tank dresses, and no makeup. I was on a mission to figure out **what the fuck just happened to me**. I had no clue what I would find there—all I knew was that I wanted a complete do-over.

People come to Bali for all kinds of reasons. This magical place set in the heart of the Indian Ocean, just off the coast of Indonesia, is known just as much for its rich food, beautiful culture, and lush greenery as it is for its beaches. For years, Australians have flocked to Bali's waters in droves to surf the epic waves, communal bonfires, and endless nights of drinking and partying.

Me? I'd come to Bali to find answers.

I had never been before, but many years ago, I read Elizabeth Gilbert's *New York Times* bestseller, *Eat Pray Love*, a book about one woman's journey to put her life back together after a divorce. The book would lead to Bali becoming the destination of pilgrimages for many women in crisis. I was self-admittedly in crisis, so I thought, why not go to Bali and figure out who I was and why I never felt like I had, or was, enough? So, the day after finishing my cancer treatments, I booked a ticket and began my journey of self-discovery.

I had no idea how I ended up here—thirty-six years old with breast cancer and no family history of the disease. I was in pretty good shape, especially for my age. For the last few years, I had eaten a mostly vegetarian diet. I didn't smoke. I worked out regularly. So, after being a picture of health, how did I get breast cancer? It's a question I still can't answer with certainty, to this very day. But if I had to guess, I'd say it had a lot to do with stress and the pressure I put on myself to be perfect and live my life on other people's terms. Many women are raised with the unrealistic idea of being a superwoman, wanting it all, having their cake, and eating it, too. I've pushed myself all my life to be the best, to be number one, to live up to my mother's legacy, and by some measures, I'd done it. Or so I thought.

* * *

I always say 2015 was the best and worst year of my life. On March 1st of that year, my company, Thank God It's Natural (tgin), launched in 250 Target stores. We had an incredible year, and it took the company to a whole new level. On December 16th of that same year, I was diagnosed with Stage 2 invasive ductile breast cancer.

After nine months of doctors' appointments, endless biopsies and X-rays, eight rounds of chemo, thirty-three rounds of radiation, five to six trips to my therapist, a lumpectomy, and freezing my eggs, my company was somehow still intact.

I, however, was a complete and utter mess. It was like I had fought in a war, only to come home and be thrust back into my old reality with a major case of PTSD. Nothing felt normal. Cancer treatment was grueling, not just physically, but also mentally and emotionally. Even though I had a pretty positive experience while undergoing treatment, with every test, X-ray, and biopsy, I was waiting on pins and needles to know whether everything was all clear, whether the cancer was responding to treatment, or even worse, whether it had spread to other parts of my body. After surviving all of that, I felt like I'd dodged a bullet. The stress was more than I could handle or even imagine.

Yet, all the tests, treatments, physical pain, and exhaustion that came with battling cancer were far more relaxing than juggling being the CEO of tgin while also working a full-time job as senior corporate counsel at Oracle, one of the world's largest software companies.

* * *

It was my last day in paradise before I headed back home to Chicago, and I had some tough decisions to make.

I sat there, looking out from my hotel room at the lush, tropical foliage that went on for miles just outside my window. I had spent days gazing at the mountains of jungle rainforest and listening to the rushing waves from the Ayung River crash against the rocks a few hundred feet below. And, on certain days, if you caught the sun at the right angle, you could see the most brilliant rainbow sparkling in the reflection of crystal-clear waterfalls. Beyond that, there was only peace. And calm. The life-altering kind of calm you never experience in your real, everyday life.

The last three weeks had been nothing short of magical. Aside from a few cultural excursions into the heart of the city of Ubud, I spent my days eating Balinese food, drinking lychee martinis, and journaling poolside as I took in the tapestry of the breathtaking landscape. If I was feeling really motivated, I would take a walk along the beach and find one of the local women sitting in a small, make-shift hut and get a soothing ninety-minute back massage for just five dollars. I needed this. The beauty of Bali. A chance to pause and reflect. A chance to breathe. This is what my soul had been crying out for these past few months, and maybe even years.

For once, I was able to hear myself think and enjoy a kind of stillness that can only be found when you go off the grid. You can't even begin to imagine what life is like when you're not constantly consuming the false reality that is pumped through social media feeds, the latest political antics, or the story of yet another innocent black man losing his life at the hands of an "I was afraid for my life" police officer. Instead, in Bali, you have nothing, no one but a few sweet-faced Balinese who greet you with a warm smile and speak the few words of broken English they know. You can't put a price tag on that kind of peace; it's invaluable.

Even with all of this harmony surrounding me, I knew it was time to make a choice. The last day of my trip had arrived. Should I stay an extra week? An extra month? Or should I say "peace out" to the craziness that was await-ing me back home and start fresh here on this little island on the other side of the world?

Here I was on the other side of cancer, with a new slate, a

clean bill of health, and a fresh start. Would I go back to who I was and continue to chase money, men, and fame, or would I really use this time to figure out my "why" and my true God-given purpose?

I was scheduled to go back to work at Oracle a week after my return from Bali. After being diagnosed with breast cancer, I had taken a leave of absence from practicing corporate law to focus solely on my health and keeping my company afloat. Now that I was "cured" and the doctors had declared me cancer-free, it was time to get back on the grind. I thought it would be easy. I had dealt with other crises before, like losing my mom to cancer right after graduating from high school and the unnerving struggles that come with building a business, but somehow, I always managed to pull it together quickly and get back to my "normal." So naturally, I thought I would be able to seamlessly transition from cancer patient to cancer survivor. Unfortunately, that was not the case. My battle with cancer at such a young age not only taught me that life was short and precious, but it dealt a major blow to my sense of security. I was no longer a superwoman.

The day I left for Bali, I checked my Oracle work email as I was heading to the airport. I hadn't been into the office in almost nine months, and sitting in my inbox were thousands upon thousands of unread emails. As I quickly skimmed through them to see if I missed anything important, one email immediately caught my eye. It was from the general counsel informing our department that a woman in the office had died after battling breast cancer. I can't describe the sudden "oh shit" moment that erupted inside me. I knew I had to make some changes. Just weeks before, I had been struggling with when to quit my day job and focus on tgin full time. Right then and there, a voice inside me was telling me I couldn't go back to operating at that level—to who and what I'd been before.

As much as I wanted to stay in this newfound wonderland, the reality was that I had a mortgage to pay, a job to start, and a company to run on the other side of the world. My employees, many of whom had built careers with the company, were counting on me. I was faced with an odd contrast as I peered at the jungle beyond my windowsill. I knew back home in Chicago lay the real jungle, filled with endless concrete, towering skyscrapers, rumbling traffic, roaring horns, and earth-shaking subways. I was always running from one event to the next, preparing for the next speech, going over my endless to-do list, solving factory issues, or meeting up with a girlfriend for brunch and drinks. Daily, I battled the constant stress and warfare of growing my business. Decisions had to be made in milliseconds, calls had to be answered, emails needed responding to. And I always had to be "on." Hair done, nails done, everything done. It was too much.

But not here in Bali. There was no schedule to keep, no event I was scheduled to speak at, no inbox of emails to respond to, no one to look good for. Nothing mattered.

I didn't know what I'd find in this mecca for the broken and lost—or whether the myth and lore surrounding it would help me find myself. The only thing I did know for sure was that I never wanted to leave.

As I continued to deliberate on whether to stay or go, I couldn't stop thinking about an encounter I'd had earlier that morning. I went to visit a spiritual reader who was recommended to me by one of my girlfriends who had visited Bali the month before.

To meet with this reader, I traveled to Kuta, a town known for its surf-friendly beaches and wild parties. She owned a cute little restaurant right off the beaten path. When we sat down for my reading, she pulled out her deck of cards. I was a bit skeptical. Her card reading abilities seemed less than average compared with other readings I'd had before. Forty-five minutes into the session, after hearing a stream of one wrong thing after another, I was ready to walk out and say, "Thanks lady. Keep the $40." But as they say, "In for a dime, in for a dollar." She suddenly said something that struck a chord.

"Chris-Tia, you're an empath," she said. "You're also

extremely intuitive. You have a gift; you just need to use it." I had always known that I was intuitive, but I never fully trusted or gave much credence to my intuition.

In the past, that voice would always be like a soft whisper in my ear. It would tell me over and over again, "That girl is not your friend," "That guy is running games," "You need to release this product." When it came to business, I always listened. When it came to personal matters, I rarely did. After years of being a lawyer and hanging out with Harvard folks, I always felt compelled to make a case for why I felt what I felt with data, witnesses, exhibits, footnotes, etc. It could be about the simplest of things, but I was always forced to offer up support or a complete analysis for what I was thinking or feeling. That dulled my intuition over time. But like Dorothy in *The Wizard of Oz*, this woman was my own personal Glinda the Good Witch, telling me that my ruby slippers were my intuition and that I had the power to go home—or be who I wanted to be—all along.

As she continued flipping the cards, she asked me about the details of my trip. I revealed to her my desire to move to Bali and leave my old life behind. She responded with words that have stuck with me to this day.

"Look, girl. It's not about Bali the place. It's about finding the Bali within you."

That's where my journey took a turn.

The rest of the day, I kept thinking about what she said. What did it mean to find the Bali within? What was it about this place that I loved so much? I started to realize that it wasn't about selling all my stuff back home and leaving my old life behind to move to Bali. It was about truly looking at my life and finding peace with who I was, what I had, and where I stood, no matter where I lived.

So many times, I traveled to places around the world, looking for an escape from the stress that came in my everyday life. I was committed to the idea of taking regular vacations, but she helped me realize that vacation is truly a state of mind rather than a particular place. How many times have I traveled to Mexico, Jamaica, Vietnam, Greece, Italy, South Africa, you name it, only to come home and feel like I needed another vacation two weeks later? I realized that if I were truly going to make it through this thing called life, I would have to be able to create peace in my daily life. I had to make it a life I wanted to come home to, a life that I felt relaxed in, a life that had more meaning than just being a CEO.

As I continued to process her words, I realized that finding the Bali within meant being grateful and staying present. I needed to create boundaries for myself, spend time with the ones I love, and ultimately, find peace within me, my home, my heart, and my spirit.

She may not have been able to predict my future or tell me if I was going to get married, but she gave me a piece of advice that will stick with me forever. That short visit with her ended up being the best forty dollars I ever spent.

Chapter Two

THE D

When I tell people I grew up in Detroit, without fail, they have one of two reactions. The first is, "No way. You didn't really grow up in Detroit. Are you really from Southfield?" The second is, "How did someone who grew up in Detroit get into Harvard?"

Detroit is an interesting place. When people think of Detroit, images immediately come to mind of vacant lots, five-dollar houses, Devil's Night, and former hip-hop mayor Kwame Kilpatrick, who is now serving a twenty-seven-year sentence for public corruption—God bless his soul. Yes, Detroit is all those things, but we're also known as the home of the Motown sound, which gave birth to the careers of Diana Ross and the Supremes, Martha and the Vandellas, and Smokey Robinson. We are Eminem and *8 Mile*, Joe Louis, and the auto industry.

Most people wouldn't know this, but Detroit actually has some of the most beautiful homes in the country. As with every city, there are good neighborhoods and bad neighborhoods, high-end areas and places where you have no business being after dark. Detroit is no different. People underestimate Detroit, just as they have underestimated me as a black woman.

One of the many things we continue to have in common is our unbreakable spirit. We have swag, and we own it. I've traveled to many cities across the United States and around the world, and I promise you, Detroit is like no other place I've ever been.

∗ ∗ ∗

Growing up in a predominantly black city with a black mayor gave me exposure to black lawyers, black millionaires, black doctors, black leadership, and black people who were simply doing well for themselves. Seeing black people run their own show, at least on a local level, shaped my outlook on the world and gave me a tremendous amount of confidence, as well as the belief that I could do anything and be anything.

For the young folks reading this, a black mayor was a big deal, no, a *huge* deal in the 1970s. Coleman Young (Detroit, 1973), Maynard Jackson (Atlanta, 1973), Tom

Bradley (Los Angeles, 1973), and Harold Washington (Chicago, 1983) were pioneers and raised the bar and the sights of what black people could become and achieve. Growing up with Young, Jackson, Bradley, and Washington shining a light was like growing up with Barack Obama for many young black people of that time.

But, in my life and in my home, the influence and mindset of overcoming didn't begin with whomever sat in the mayor's seat. It started with my parents.

MARIE

My mom, Marie Farrell-Donaldson, was born in Detroit and was the first black woman to be certified as a public accountant in the state of Michigan, which was major back in the 1970s. She had an amazing career holding high-level government positions in what was then a thriving Detroit in the midst of transitioning from white to black leadership.

My mom grew up poor and was the first person in her family to earn a college degree. Despite the fact that my grandmother was a housewife with a high school education, she always impressed upon her children the importance of getting their degree, and three of her four children ended up going to college. The fourth earns six figures working in an auto parts factory.

She somehow managed to put herself through college by working at a grocery store. One fateful day she went to her college counselor to inquire about choosing a profession. She informed them that she wanted to major in accounting but was told that women didn't major in accounting and that she should consider teaching instead. In her usual fashion, she didn't pay any mind to what people told her she couldn't do. She did what she wanted to, graduated with a degree in accounting and finance, and went on to become a pioneer for black women in Michigan's accounting industry.

Shortly after earning her degree, she married her college sweetheart, a Kappa by the name of Joe Farrell. They divorced just a year later, which would leave her as a single mom to my sister, Piper. Like most recently divorced women, she struggled financially to make it on her own. Since she was just getting her start as an accountant, she went to the public aid office to get assistance with caring for my sister. As the story goes, my mom showed up at the welfare office first thing in the morning, but when the clerk told her she was going to need to bring her lunch because she would be there all day, my mother made the decision right there on the spot to leave and never look back. Instead of waiting on someone to give her money, she set out to make her own.

Throughout her early twenties, she fought to gain her

footing professionally, as no accounting firm would take the chance of hiring a young black woman. The lack of opportunities ultimately required her to start her own firm, with my grandmother being her sole financial backer.

Over the years, she earned a reputation for doing good work, and by the young age of twenty-seven, she became the first female auditor general and, later, ombudsman of the City of Detroit. This was quite an accomplishment for someone her age. As a result, she was often featured in various local and national publications and was even personally invited to the White House by Presidents Ronald Reagan and George Bush for her role in creating a more accountable government.

Most days during my childhood, my dad would pick me up from school and drop me off at my mom's office. Now that I'm older, I realize how impactful it was for me to grow up watching my mom lead a staff of fifteen employees. Seeing a woman like her be in charge became my norm; I knew nothing else. She backed down to no one, including the mayor of the City of Detroit, whom she regularly went head to head with on various political issues. And as a young child, she showed me how to be strong, no-nonsense, and fearless; she would ultimately become my reference point for letting people know I was not to be played with, all the while maintaining the image of grace under pressure.

After my mom got off work in the evenings, she was understandably exhausted. We would often laugh that dinner was sometimes a combination of Swedish meatballs and chicken wings, a common staple at receptions and cocktail parties that were hosted by local businesspeople and elected officials, including my mother. To this day, my schedule looks almost the same, but I don't have a daughter to tag along as my mini-me. Still, my mom was an incredible cook, and when she did have the time to spend in the kitchen, she would pull out all the stops and make sure our favorites were always prepared with love.

If there is one thing I remember the most about her, it was that she had phenomenal fashion sense. Unlike me, she took tremendous pride in her appearance and made a point to put on a nice dress or suit every single day for work. If she loved anything, it was when the Michigan weather dropped below freezing. That's when she had the opportunity to rock her furs—full length, waist length, mink, and beaver—to show she had made it.

She was proud of her wardrobe that she found at quaint boutiques in hidden enclaves throughout the city. Again, this was Detroit in the eighties, and everyone thought they were high couture, shopping for clothes in stores that carried unique pieces with limited availability. This was back when shoulder pads, giant necklaces, sequins, and long, flowing tunics with hand-painted and bejeweled adornments were in. Truth be told, you'll still find many sisters over forty back in the D rocking these items to this day as if they have not gone out of style. There is no way you're telling them they are not Black Queens.

As one of the few black women with blond hair in Detroit in the eighties, my mom was often asked who her colorist was. But she refused to tell anyone her secret, including her own hair dresser, as she had adeptly mastered the art of mixing salon-grade chemicals to bleach and dye her own hair with the results being the perfect shade of honey blond. This was before Dark & Lovely came out with high-lift blond box color, so going blond as a black woman in the 1980s was considered a major accomplishment, especially if you managed to maintain a head full of healthy hair.

Although she never forgot where she came from, she and many other blacks from that generation took tremendous pride in the fact that they were indeed "moving on up," just like the Jeffersons. Still, beneath the carefully curated exterior was a woman who was not only humble but loving, kind, and of tremendous moral character. She was a confident and take-charge woman in the professional realm but provided a great example of how to fall back at home and let my dad take charge and feel like the king of the castle.

CLINT

My dad, Clinton Lavonne Donaldson, hails from David-son, North Carolina. Like many blacks, he moved to the north after leaving the Air Force in hopes of finding more opportunity as part of the Great Migration. When he landed in Detroit, he was among the first group of African Americans selected to join the Detroit Police Department after the death of civil rights leader, Martin Luther King, Jr. After building an excellent reputation on the police force, my dad eventually rose to the top of the department, earning the rank of commander and becoming the head of Internal Affairs. This was a major deal, considering the force had been largely white for years. In this role, he oversaw major investigations involving corruption within the ranks, including high profile murder and drug cases, which included major gangs, like Young Boys Incorporated. Given his detective skills, telling a lie or trying to pull one past my dad growing up got me absolutely nowhere.

Like my mom, he had an appreciation for the finer things in life, considering he didn't come from much. On most days, you could catch him dressed to the nines in a custom-tailored suit, butterscotch Italian leather shoes, a trench coat, and a black fedora hat. My parents were both Leos, with birthdays five days apart from one another, so their love for nice clothes, luxury cars, and shiny things was not unusual. Plus, everyone was extra in the eighties.

After leaving the police department, my dad went on to get his PhD, teach at the local university, and work as an expert witness for wrongful death cases. As a product of the segregated South, he saw where education could take you and always impressed that upon me. Given his law enforcement training, he was, and still is, very methodical. Any time I ask him for advice, he is never quick to respond. Instead, he will call me days later, long after I have forgotten what we were talking about, with a fully researched answer, including a scripture. Of all the men I've ever come across, he is by far the most religious in the sense that he grew up strongly rooted in the church and reads his Bible every morning. I get my attention to detail, my hazel eyes, and, he would say, my brains from him, although my mom would beg to differ.

My parents, like most parents in the eighties, weren't the most affectionate people, but I knew they loved me. I had a really good childhood. I got enough hugs, and they often told me they loved me and were proud of me. They came to my recitals, programs, and parent-teacher conferences, but I could tell they were most proud of me when I came home with all As. So much so that I think my unhealthy obsession with success and accomplishment ties back to the feeling of being loved when I made good grades as a child.

Overall, though, I don't have any real complaints about

my childhood other than I wish my mom was around a lot more, especially given that our time together was so limited.

GRANDMA LOLO

If I were to describe my mom as high maintenance, my Grandma Lolo was the complete opposite. For most of my childhood, I can remember her sitting comfortably on the couch in the front room, wearing nothing but her bra and a pair of jogging pants. The phone was always pressed to her ear for hours while she caught up on *Young & the Restless*. When she wasn't busy watching a house full of badass grandkids who were setting the carpet on fire—guilty as charged—or playing Cowboys and Indians with my grandad's loaded shotgun, you could find her leading Bible study, ushering at a funeral, or doing missionary work in the community.

Over the years, she filled me and my cousins with a lifetime of black grandma-isms, like "If you gon' be something, be the best," "You attract more flies with honey than you do with vinegar," "Never tell a man everything," and "If you sleep with a man, make him pay for it, even if it's just a quarter." Her advice, both solicited and unsolicited, always came from a place of love and played a major part in shaping me into the businesswoman I am today. She never hid her truth or tried to protect me from the harsh realities that came with being a black woman in America.

My grandma married my grandfather, Herman Morgan, when she was just eighteen and lived in Virginia Park for nearly her entire adult life until she died in 2018. The neighborhood had once been home to a thriving working-class community, but by the 1980s, it had fallen into decay due to the proliferation of crack and other drugs in parts of the inner city. There were plenty of abandoned houses on her block, a huge vacant lot across the street, trap houses down the road, and Lord knows what else going on. Despite its steady decline, I spent a significant amount of time at my grandparents' house after school and on weekends because my mother traveled a lot for work. Unlike other kids in the neighborhood, my cousins and I were only allowed to play on one end of the block. Crossing the street or going to the corner store was absolutely out of the question.

I was quick to call Lolo's house my second home. It was filled with love and lots of cousins, uncles, and aunts coming and going at all hours of the day. My fondest memories growing up are of me and my cousins spending Friday nights watching *Family Matters* and eating a bucket of fried chicken from KFC. A close second would be running outside from her no-air-conditioning sweatbox of a house into the sweltering heat of a hundred-plus-degree summer's day to chase down the ice cream truck as its chiming bells drove down the street.

My grandmother kept a tight grip and a protective eye on me and my other girl cousins in particular. If there was anything she was concerned about, it was us getting pregnant. Through one part scare tactic, one part intimidation, she made it her personal mission to keep me a virgin as long as possible. As a result, when I was younger, I always found myself having to explain to my guy friends why they couldn't sit on the porch or stand in front of her house and why they had to hang up if she answered the phone when they called the house to talk. My grandma was old school, which meant it was her house and her "crazy" rules. But, hey, they worked.

My grandma's house and the childhood friends I made over the years would give me an up-close glimpse of what it was like to not have a lot. In Virginia Park, I had to be able to make friends with people from all economic backgrounds. I had to be okay with people saying I talked white, while still playing Hands Up for 85 with the best of them. I never viewed myself as having two identities or felt I had to apologize for living on the nice side of town; I just had to keep it real. That's how it goes down in the D.

Spending so much time in Virginia Park is part of the reason why I am where I am today. While a lot of people "make it" and want to associate only with those who are successful or have the same amount of resources that they do, I have found that my ability to work closely with and be an advocate for individuals across all socio-economic backgrounds has been critical to my success. I always tell people I would never have been able to get tgin off the ground if it weren't for the people without college degrees who were willing to put in long hours and work for minimum wage to help lay the foundation for what we have built today.

* * *

My parents made huge sacrifices to send me to private school in the suburbs, where I got an excellent education. If it weren't for Gibson School for the Gifted, I don't know if I would be who I am today. It was there that I learned to question authority, challenge assumptions, and tap into my creativity. We even called our teachers by their first names. It was at this school that my intellectual curiosity and independent personality was fully nurtured. Whether it was trips to the Detroit Institute of Arts to learn about Diego Rivera, studying Bach's compositions, or camping in the woods, Gibson opened my world and taught me to love and appreciate learning.

While I knew I went to a school for the gifted, I didn't know exactly what that meant, only that we were smart, and our education was different. There I was, this little black girl who was a voracious reader learning about Salvador Dalí and advanced geometry at a very young age.

Naturally, I was very competitive as a child and always wanted to win. Whether it was pull-ups in a presidential fitness challenge or scoring a perfect score on an algebra test, I wanted to be number one. My parents often viewed my accomplishments, big and small, as their own. I wanted to make them proud, so I kept striving for excellence. Looking back, I realize I put a lot of that pressure on myself, a trait that would follow me into adulthood.

Despite the phenomenal education and fond memories I have of my early education, I longed for something more. From second through eighth grade, I was the only black girl in my class. I wanted to be around kids and teachers who looked like me. My parents didn't have a real sense of the impact that world had on me. They'd grown up in all-black, segregated schools during the Civil Rights Era. The world of an all-white school was beyond their experience and understanding. They simply believed in the importance of a good education and provided me with the best their money could buy.

It was an indescribable feeling, but I always felt like something was off or missing. Although I never had a hard time making friends or fitting in, I never truly felt "at home" in this all-white environment. Part of this had to do with hair and beauty. Back then, the world was a very different place. This was back when blond hair and blue eyes were in style and the ultimate beauty standards. And this was definitely before "black girl magic" and "melanin poppin'" were a thing. It was rare to see black girls on the cover of major national magazines, other than *Ebony*, *Jet*, and *Essence*.

I had no problem fitting in socially with my white classmates. Yet, sometimes my kinky hair made me feel like a complete and total outsider. It was one thing to grow up watching white sitcoms from the 1980s, like *The Wonder Years*, *Family Ties,* and *Growing Pains*, but it was another story to go to school every day and be surrounded by a sea of white girls with flowing hair that hung down their backs. In contrast to their beautiful, blond, shimmering tresses, my short, brown hair seemed so dull and ugly.

To make matters worse, my cornrows with aluminum foil and colored beads on the ends made me stick out like a sore thumb. At this point, no one had seen or even heard of Venus and Serena Williams, so there was no way I could possibly play this ethnic style off as cool. My cornrows were convenient and kept me from fussing with my hair, but I secretly wished for long, blond tresses that I could squirt pink L.A. gel in and pull back into a scrunchie. I survived all of this, of course, but I was deeply impacted and emotionally scarred for years to come. This longing to physically blend in with my white female classmates coupled with a persistent feeling of dissatisfaction with my own appearance would prove to be the beginning of a decade-long battle with my hair and my coming to grips with who I was as a black woman. Though this wasn't an earth-shattering or violent experience, feeling out of place—see: *ethnic*—certainly left me doubting my self-image and my beauty as a black woman.

Going to a predominantly white school taught me how important diversity is to the education process. Gibson was one of my first introductions into being a black woman in a largely all-white space, which rarely left me feeling at peace with who I was. My early childhood experiences, however, would serve me well many years later when it came to being a black woman in the predominantly white, male-dominant legal profession. It would also lay the foundation for why I went on to start my own hair company, Thank God It's Natural (tgin).

* * *

After graduating from Gibson, I spent the next four years at Mercy High School, an all-girls high school. When I entered Mercy, its name signified so much for me. The mercy of Mercy High School was its diversity. There were forty black girls in my class of two hundred. We made up almost a quarter of the class. I soon discovered a strong black community and had the opportunity to experience a real sisterhood.

Since my parents were on the "no sleepover at your friend's house" program when I was growing up, high school was truly one of the first times that I really got to interact with my classmates outside of school. Many of my closest friends were like sisters. Even though we looked nothing alike, you knew we hung together from our matching black leather coats, dolphin gold earrings, crimped hairstyles, dark auburn Wet *n* Wild lipstick (#508), and too much black eyeliner. It was the 90s, and you couldn't tell us anything. If we weren't hanging out at the mall, you could find us at our brother school's basketball games, on the phone, or hatching some plan to meet up with some guys at the movies.

Mercy represented a certain degree of freedom for me, and for the first time, I felt at home in an academic setting. I loved the friends I met in high school and rarely ever experienced judgment from others. I was able to show up to school however I wanted and not be subjected to constant questions about my clothes, hair, food, or anything else that seemed unusual to some. Mercy was a place where women could be close to one another, find themselves, and excel academically without the distraction of boys. Wait, let me clarify. Boys may not have been in our classes, but they were definitely always on the brain and often waiting in the parking lot at three o'clock for school to let out.

Throughout school, I was in all honors classes, and I continued to excel. During my freshman year, I earned straight As. After that, I knew nothing less would do. My dad was a man of very few words, but I knew he was proud, and he rewarded me for it. Back then, I was naïve in thinking that rewards came to those who worked hard, and that the world was a meritocracy, but that's how I motivated myself through my high school years and beyond.

At the same time, during my freshman year, my sister, who was a senior at the University of Michigan, got married and started a family in her final semester of college. Although she would later go on to earn her PhD and be extremely successful, seeing her struggle emotionally and financially to make her marriage work at a young age was not lost on me. In my family, I was raised to want babies, but there was an inordinate amount of pressure to focus on school, get an education, get a good job, make a lot of money, and then—when life was "under control"—start a family. I think seeing my sister deal with the challenges that marriage and motherhood brought was also a contributing factor to why I delayed having a family of my own and why I opted to remain laser focused on my career at the expense of relationships and everything else.

During my junior year of high school, my mom ran for the US House of Representatives. Although she lost the election, it was an exciting time for women in politics and showed me what I could one day accomplish. Six months after the campaign ended, my mom was diagnosed with non-Hodgkin's lymphoma. It was March of 1995. When I say no one in my family has had cancer, I mean no one. She was the first. After losing the election and being diagnosed with cancer, my mom decided she wanted to move to the suburbs and live in a house on the water, so we moved. Maybe she knew she was dying, but I doubt she did. Everything just seemed so normal.

I was just sixteen at the time, and given my strong academic performance in school, my parents didn't really opt to share much, if anything, with me. I just knew my mom was sick. I learned that she would need a bone marrow transplant but had no clue what that meant. I don't even remember seeing my mom with a cold during that time. Other than seeing her lose her hair and wear a wig, everything was normal. She got up, put on her suit, her wig, and makeup, and went to work every single day. When I say every single day, I mean every single day. She literally never missed a beat.

Back then, there was no Google. I had nowhere to turn for answers, so I just trusted whatever information my parents shared with me and assumed everything would be alright. I didn't really know much about what her condition meant or what the prognosis was. There was no question that my mom would simply get better.

While my mom underwent treatment, I continued to be a typical teenage girl, focusing on my school work and applying to college. By my senior year, I had continued to maintain a straight-A average and set my eyes on going to the Ivy League. With the strong influence of my mom's background in politics and government, I set my sights on Yale, a school known for its commitment to public service and the production of some of our nation's top lawyers and judges. Again, this was before the internet. Back then, we had to decide where to attend college based on the catalogues mailed to us from different universities, movies like *School Daze,* and TV shows like *A Different World*.

I remember asking my AP biology teacher to write me a recommendation letter for the Ivy League schools I planned on applying to. He replied by saying, "No. You don't know how to talk, and you aren't ready for schools like Harvard and Yale." At the time, I thought he was joking because I had the second highest grade in his class, and it seemed like he actually liked me. But he was dead serious. This was the same teacher who, after we moved to West Bloomfield, a posh suburb just outside of Detroit, asked me if my parents were drug dealers.

Those comments stung at the time, but only in hindsight do I now see how deeply rooted they are in racism. Sometimes people are threatened by your strength and abilities even when you're much younger than them, and this man was one of those people. My conversation with this teacher was one of my first major encounters with the micro-aggression that comes with being black and smart in America, and it certainly wouldn't be my last. His words planted a seed and caused me to work even harder while I learned to navigate predominantly white spaces that refused to celebrate black excellence.

* * *

Around spring break of my senior year, my mother learned that she would need a bone marrow transplant. Finding a donor for minorities can be especially difficult, but my mom's sister proved to be an identical match. Against doctors' orders, she delayed having the transplant so she could make it to my high school prom and graduation.

I'm glad she did. Our time shopping together for my prom dress is a memory that I'm forever thankful for. After heading to multiple stores and trying on several different numbers, we settled on a beautiful, lilac, off-the-shoulder, tea-length dress with a sheer bottom. To this day, I look back on that dress and think about how beautiful and timeless it was. The same was true for graduation. At

Mercy, we wore floor-length, white dresses and carried twelve red roses at graduation. After searching high and low for a graduation dress, we found a beautiful white wedding dress with a flowy, tulle bottom and a detailed flowery corset top. It was absolutely stunning. I'm not much of a girly girl, and I've never been married, but shopping for my graduation dress would be the closest I got to picking out a wedding dress with my mom. It's a memory I will always cherish.

Back then, I never saw my mom's death coming. No one did. My mom was my rock, which is why it came as a complete and total shock. She was my Superwoman. I had never known anyone diagnosed with cancer and wasn't aware that the disease could be fatal. I had such a limited view of death at that point that I couldn't even begin to process the idea of losing my mom.

Growing up, it's perfectly normal to think your parents are going to grow old and live to be seventy-five. Up until then, things pretty much worked out the way they were supposed to. However, this time, they didn't. On June 29, 1996, my sister called me and told me our mother was gone. It is a day I'll never forget. Losing my mom to cancer was one of my first and greatest tests. Losing a loved one is painful; the loss of a mother is indescribable. It felt like someone literally ripped my heart out of my chest and stabbed it a thousand times. It's the kind of pain that not even a bottle of pills and a fifth of vodka can soothe. There's no other way to describe it. It was like I was having a nightmare and was just hoping that when I woke up, someone would be there to tell me it was all just a bad dream. I'm still waiting.

I was numb with disbelief in the days shortly after her passing. I was surrounded by family and friends during the time leading up to the funeral. There was a steady influx of hugs, kisses, and cards to help take my mind off my loss, but when the funeral had passed and friends and relatives had gone back to living their respective lives, I was left alone with no one but myself and my thoughts. In those moments, it was easy for my mind to wander into dark places that had me thinking about doing things that I may not even have the opportunity to regret. It was like there was a hole in me that nothing could ever fill. I learned that no amount of people, boyfriends, girlfriends, drinks, sex, or work could ever fill the void that was missing in my life.

Back then—and even somewhat today—therapy was seen as taboo and was not fully embraced by the black community. As a child, I grew up watching my mom and grandmother pray and lean on the cross to get through life's most difficult circumstances. So, at no point during the aftermath of my mother's passing did anyone suggest that I see a counselor. I didn't have any example or model for dealing with this kind of tragedy, so I turned to work. That summer, before heading off to college, I got a second job as a waitress at a local restaurant for fun, supplementing the money I was making working for a law clerk at a local attorney's office. I would file social security claims by day and serve customers their burgers and fries at night. When I got home around 10 p.m., I would close the door to my room and cry myself to sleep.

My dad was extremely young during this ordeal and had to process not only the loss of his wife and best friend but also find a way to prepare emotionally, mentally, and financially to send his daughter off to college more than two thousand miles away in less than sixty days. I should have been excited about going away to school, but it just wasn't the same without my mom there. As the days came closer for heading off to Cambridge, I started looking forward to getting out of the house where my mom once lived in exchange for a new environment where I wouldn't have to deal with the daily reminder of my loss.

A friend of the family suggested that I take a year off to focus on myself. I never gave serious consideration to the idea of taking a break because, to me, that would have been like failing. I had been accepted to the number one university in the nation and, in some cases, depending on who you talk to, the world. This was something I had worked hard for, and remember, my accomplishments also belonged to my parents. I couldn't blow it, especially when I was raised by a woman who had accomplished so much. It was a lot to take in, a lot of pressure.

Throughout my childhood, my mom was always a model of strength. When I dealt with small setbacks over the years, she didn't simply encourage me but, rather, forced me to push through them. If I cried because I lost a tennis match or a math competition, there weren't a lot of hugs, but she never failed to tell me that I was unbreakable and possibly needed to try harder next time. When my mom lost her race for Congress, she was up the next day handling business as usual. When she got cancer, she kept going. This strength was the blueprint for my life.

The summer after my mom's passing, I really had to get to know my dad. Even though we lived in the same house during my upbringing, I was always closer to my mom. Anything he needed to know would generally be filtered through her. He was constantly present and a good provider, but we didn't say much to each other. Still, I knew he loved me. But in those days before I left for college, a seed was planted, and we grew closer than ever. This man of few words would later become my best friend, confidant, spiritual advisor, and later, honorary chairman of tgin's board.

Chapter Three

HARVARD

In August of 1996, my dad and I packed up the car and made the eleven-hour drive to Cambridge, Massachusetts, where he dropped me off at freshman orientation. He often tells me that, to this day, leaving me there was one of the hardest things he's ever had to do, especially considering he had to go back to an empty house.

In life—as a child, a teen, and now as an adult—I learned to always keep pushing forward, no matter the circumstances. There was no time for rest. There was no time for reflection. There was no time for tears. During this extremely difficult time, my grandmother, God bless her soul, implored me to cut out all that crying, because I had to be grateful for the family I had left. I just had to keep going, and that's what I did. While I had given myself sixty days to deal with the fact that I had lost my mom, I had to move on, leave it behind, and start school. I thought that was more than enough time. *Life happens*, or so I thought. With this being my first exposure to a major trauma, the only thing I knew how to do was bury it.

This experience of loss became my ultimate reference point for dealing with difficult moments, be it break-ups, rejection letters, business issues, or what have you. I would just bury my pain and move on. I thought I had to push the feelings down deep inside so I could carry on as a functional human being. It had the exact opposite effect. Instead, I had become hyper-focused on my work and my studies in an effort to tune out the feelings boiling up inside and the emotional baggage I was not prepared to deal with.

I went on to spend the next seven years of my life in Cambridge, majoring in economics as an undergraduate and then earning my law degree from Harvard Law School. One of my greatest fears during my time in college was having a nervous breakdown and needing to drop out. This fear was compounded by the fact that although Harvard doesn't put a lot of pressure on its students, it does have a lot of extremely smart, super driven, type-A personalities in one place. I never really felt like I was in competition with anyone, but it wasn't unusual for people to take time off for "personal reasons." Taking time off came with a certain stigma at Ivy Leagues. Many people believed that those students were unable to handle the pressure of such a highly selective environment. I was determined to work even harder to make sure my grades were solid. I was certain it was more than just what my mom would have wanted. It was my destiny to excel.

There I was, not only dealing with the emotional issues that came with losing my mom, but I was going to college in New England, which was home to people like Mitt Romney, the Kennedys, and the Forbes. My classmates were the children of senators, Wall Street investment bankers, captains of industry, foreign diplomats, and African royalty. Being there meant you were handpicked to change the world. You were being groomed to be among our nation's leaders. I realized quickly that I had to come to terms with my own identity—a seventeen-year-old black girl from Detroit in the midst of a prominent, diverse but predominantly white, space.

Harvard was incredible, almost magical. Its rich history dates back to 1636, and it has the coins to back it up. The streets were cobblestone, like something you would have seen during the American Revolution. The dorms at that time, though renovated and equipped with fireplaces, have also remained intact since the eighteenth century. The students were some of the most brilliant and talented people I have ever surrounded myself with—chess masters, published authors, and master concerto violinists.

There were tuxedo dances, lobster nights in the dining hall, and people like Will Smith, Jada Pinkett, Halle Berry, and then-Senator Barack Obama visiting the campus to give lectures and meet with students. The place held a strong sense of tradition, and although I was surrounded by this sea of white upper-class privilege, I never felt like I didn't belong.

I was a black female student at a college that had only started admitting women twenty years earlier, in 1977. Still, I knew this was a test I would pass. It was a test to see whether I could survive in this world that was so different from the one I grew up in, one that would teach me how to live life by my own rules.

It was the first time I felt ordinary; I wasn't a chess master or the daughter of a wealthy socialite like many of the other students on campus, but I was well-rounded with exceptional social skills, and that was enough for me. I decided to use my time there as an opportunity to thrive. I had to adopt the mindset of "when in Rome, do as the Romans do," in clothes, in speech, in behaviors, and in attitude.

I knew I hadn't started in the same place as other students, but instead of focusing on where I began, I focused on where I wanted to be.

People often ask me if Harvard was difficult academically.

I tell them it was never about the books; it was always about money, power, and relationships. The hardest part was getting in. While Yale has always had a strong reputation for producing graduates who went into public service, the majority of my Harvard classmates, while concerned about various causes, were focused much more on lucrative-paying careers or marrying people who were highly compensated. Despite our differences in background, when it came to race or geography, it seemed like most people there were driven to achieve a higher social and economic status. This wasn't true for everyone, but I encountered far more social climbers there than any other environment I have been in as adult.

At Harvard, no one ever talked about money, but there was always this underlying feeling that people were trying to gauge your economic status, how important you were, or whether you would become the next fill-in-the-blank. No one ever came out and asked how much money your parents had, but people were able to pick up on social cues. A person may casually mention their vacation home in the Hamptons, skiing in Sun Valley, their grandfather who owned a steel company, or that their parents belonged to the same country club as the president. It was a master class, and I was taking notes. I would learn much later that Harvard was really a training ground for understanding how privileged society determines who they choose to associate with, do business with, take in, or mentor. To be honest, this was far more common among my white classmates than my black ones, but it was all very calculated. I had an up-close seat, right behind home plate, for all of it.

Relationships were important, and a great deal of emphasis was put on socializing and joining private societies with the goal of building lifelong networks that would help students professionally after graduation. During my time at Harvard, I pledged Alpha Kappa Alpha Sorority Incorporated and joined the Bee Club, an invitation-only social club whose membership was made up largely of the school's wealthiest, prettiest, and most influential women. After some time, I ended up being elected as the president of this prestigious club. In my experience, serious romantic relationships, especially among black students, were also very rare. The campus fully embraced a "hookup culture" where dating was merely a one-night transaction. On a few occasions, though, college sweethearts married and remain together to this day.

Still, Harvard was a place where people were passionate about everything, be it music, theater, the arts, science, or public service. Being passionate about something meant they weren't just good at it, they were great at it. There was always a protest of some sort or a cause that students were fighting for, whether it was animal rights, higher wages for university employees, summer mentoring programs for underprivileged kids, divestiture in South Africa, or transgender awareness. That intensity rubbed off on me along the way, and hair and natural beauty became a growing passion for me that took on a life of its own.

I always get asked, *"What are the black folks like at Harvard?"* When I visited the campus for the very first time, I saw so many smart, beautiful, and cool black people just like me. I knew in my heart Harvard was where I was meant to be. My black classmates came from everywhere—the Bay, Baltimore, Miami, New York, Iowa, and everywhere in between. There were those of us who went to elite private boarding schools, like Andover and Phillips Exeter, and those who graduated from inner-city public schools. Although we came from different backgrounds, both geographically and economically, the community was almost instantly connected the moment you stepped on campus. Yes, there were the few "incogs" who wouldn't give the requisite head nod when you passed each other in the Yard, or those who would go out of their way to avoid anything having to do with "black students," but for the most part, everyone was down and somehow connected to the Black Students Association, the Association of Black Harvard Women, or one of the historically black Greek letter organizations.

What I was not expecting was for black people to be from

around the world. I struggled with my identity not only in terms of class, talent, and academic potential, but from a geographical standpoint. I was constantly asked where I was from by other black students, to which I would respond, "Detroit." They would look at me and ask again. I quickly learned that they were asking me what country my family's origins came from—Nigeria, Ghana, West Indies, St. Kitts, Jamaica, etc. A large number of the black students hailed from the East Coast, and many were first generation Americans, meaning their parents had immigrated to the United States, usually from the Caribbean or Africa. While I never felt ashamed of not knowing where my family came from, for the first time ever, I became aware of the fact that I didn't know my family's ancestry. Still, Detroit was, and will always be, good enough for me.

Despite our different backgrounds, it didn't matter where we came from. We were all brown, swimming in a vast sea of whiteness. Although schools like Princeton and Yale have a black house where students live or congregate, that was not the case at Harvard. We still managed to build strong relationships with our fellow black classmates through organizing and participating in major events, like our spring fashion show, step shows, gospel concerts, spur-of-the-moment rap battles, room parties, or reggae dance-offs. When one of us accomplished something major, like becoming the first black president of the Undergraduate Council, we all celebrated and rejoiced together. We were a community and are very much a family to this day.

Of all my memories from college, dinner time ranks among my fondest. Every night, I would come home after a long day on the Yard and find that one table of black students, laughing, joking, and debating everything from who was the greatest MC to whose ideology on black social progress made the greatest impact. We would literally sit in the dining hall for hours, ultimately being the last ones to leave, before we decided to make our way to the library and hit the books.

Despite being a woman and a minority, I used my time at Harvard as an opportunity to grow as an individual, learn from others, and build my network. It wouldn't be until I graduated that the challenges of being a smart, black woman in a world that's threatened by black excellence would come back to haunt me.

Chapter Four

———————

THE GAME

Growing up, I was led to believe that the worst thing that could happen to a young girl was getting pregnant out of wedlock. Not only would it bring shame on her family, but it would mean sudden death for all her hopes, dreams, and aspirations. *Get pregnant and your life is over!* It didn't stop me from gushing over boys, but the message being sent to women in my family was clear: go to school, get an education, make that money, get a husband but don't depend on him too much, always be able to take care of yourself, always keep some money hidden in a separate bank account, and everything else will be fine.

Back then, the world was a very different place. HIV was still this very scary thing, and gay marriage was pretty much unheard of. By today's standards, the world was simple, and the life we saw on TV and in magazines was pretty much what we tried to emulate. For me, this meant growing up, going to college, getting my degree, finding my "Dwayne Wayne," and starting a family because that was what I was told mattered.

No one ever told me to stop and think about what was important to me or what I thought mattered. When you grow up in a house seeing pictures of your mother shaking hands with various presidents of the United States and being celebrated for her accomplishments, it creates an unspoken standard that I only now realize. You feel an inordinate amount of pressure to top that, so to speak, because what parent doesn't want their kids to do better than they did? At a very young age, I started to believe that success was what mattered most. I chased it tirelessly, while attempting to eliminate all distractions.

My mom was my standard for womanhood. Superwoman that is. She was able to juggle being a wife and a mother, while having a career that made a difference. I grew up believing I needed to accomplish all that she did and more in order to be successful. And trust me, I've tried. As I near my fortieth birthday, I'm finally at a point where I'm starting to realize that success is not about how much money I make or how many times I get invited to the White House; it's about living life on my own terms. I respect and admire my mother for all that she was able to accomplish, but after battling cancer, I started to realize that her path was not my own. My diagnosis threw my sense of identity and my understanding of success for a loop. When I hit that time in my life, I began to realize that a lot of the decisions I had made in my life were about what made other people happy versus what actually made me happy.

Breast cancer gave me the permission I needed to do what I wanted to do, when I wanted to do it, and how I wanted to do it. When my life was hanging in the balance, I quickly learned to reshuffle the deck of life's priorities, but it still took me some time to get there.

* * *

When I was deciding what to do after graduating from college, I chose law as a career. I had watched a couple episodes of *LA Law*, and it made the life of a lawyer look pretty good. I didn't really find cases or the court experience interesting, but I loved business and found out corporate lawyers often played a role in helping businesses grow, acquire more businesses, or even sell businesses. Lawyers were respected, smart, and made a lot of money, and my favorite TV shows reinforced that on a weekly basis. Every Thursday night, Clair Huxtable would stroll ever so confidently across my screen, giving me a great role model to look up to.

Given how the world thought back then, when I graduated from college, there were three career options I could realistically consider. I could work on Wall Street and help big companies get bigger, I could go to medical school to try to cure obscure diseases, or, I could go to law school and represent big corporations that no one had heard of in litigation.

I chose option three because I was dating a cutie from Morehouse who was applying to law school. I figured, *What the heck; I'll go to law school, too.* That was the blueprint. Our grandparents followed it, our parents followed it, and now, it was my turn. If I did what I was supposed to, I would have a good job, a 401(k), and best of all, free health and dental insurance with a year's supply of contact lenses for the next forty years of my life. I'd have stability. My dad also loved telling people I was a lawyer, so my trajectory was pretty linear—always up.

The Wall Street Journal, The New York Times, and *Black Enterprise* were major publications that would highlight certain individuals making significant moves. Whether it was in finance, marketing, or government, most of these individuals were alumni of Harvard. With these individuals and my mom as reference points, it was obvious what I was supposed to amount to and to achieve. Again, I really never gave a thought to the life that I wanted to live absent of accomplishment.

Back then, entrepreneurship wasn't the hot thing it is today. Entrepreneurship was for the weird kids who couldn't get jobs or were still figuring their lives out. While I was at Harvard back in the nineties, it was illegal to start a business on campus, according to our student handbook. Students weren't allowed to use a university telephone, internet connection, or mailbox address to start a business. Those who did would face suspension or be brought before the administrative board for a hearing. To put things in perspective, there were no classes on entrepreneurship, no *Shark Tank* pitch competitions, no accelerators, and no business plan competitions. Everything was about getting a job at some large, fancy company, climbing the corporate ladder, and working for someone else. Today, young adults start businesses during or right after college because entrepreneurship is what's in now. But, in the eighties, nineties, and early 2000s, stepping off the path and going against the grain was not what the world was about.

Entrepreneurship, however unconventional, later became a big part of my life.

* * *

New York was believed to be the pinnacle of the legal profession, where all the top law firms like Skadden Arps, Cleary Gottlieb, and Cravath, Swaine & Moore were based. Many of my classmates gravitated to New York after graduation because New York law firms were "sexy," handled some of the most complex cases, and paid more to do it. But me, I wanted to be closer to home.

Although I was offered a position in New York after graduation, I accepted a role at one of the top law firms in Chicago, the one where Michelle met Barack Obama back when he was a summer intern. Though we handled all kinds of fancy lawsuits, making that particular move made me feel like I was stepping off the beaten path.

When I started my new job, I had this naïve belief that if I worked really hard, stayed longer than anyone else, put in 150 percent, and made white people feel comfortable, I would win the prize and become partner one day. By comfortable, I mean no braids, no locks, no TWA (teeny weeny Afro), no color clothes—strictly blue suit and black pumps. So, I secretly wore a wig for over a year to hide my naturally kinky hair, a concept completely unprofessional and almost unheard of in corporate America, especially in Chicago at that time. I had no other point of reference for being authentically black in corporate America, and the people giving me the little advice I got seemed to know what they were talking about. They called it "playing the game." None of these secrets to success could have been further from the truth.

My insecurities regarding my hair were deepened by the fact that I had just done the Big Chop right after my graduation from law school, and now all I had was a TWA. Wearing a short, natural style in Midwest corporate America was a major no-no. I may have been able to pull the look off at an East Coast law firm, but it was definitely not going down in Chicago. This was way before kinky, curly hair was mainstream, so many black women had to keep their natural hair on the low.

To look more polished and professional, most black women resorted to relaxing their hair. Not only did I not see any other naturals in corporate America, I didn't know the first thing about taking care of these little, tight, dry kinks and curls on my head, because products and information for natural hair weren't easily accessible during that time. There might have been a few black-owned businesses that could lend some help, but for the most part, your girl was on her own. So wearing a wig was really my only option.

To make matters worse, people were clueless about what was on my head and always complimented the health and shine of my hair. These comments made taking off my wig and showing people who I really was even harder, especially when I wasn't even comfortable with my natural hair or myself during this transition.

Not only was I dealing with the pressures of being on call

24/7 in an environment that wasn't the most diverse or hospitable to people of color, but I was also questioning my identity as a black woman working in corporate America. I thought that if I looked like a more sophisticated and polished version of Clair Huxtable from *The Cosby Show*, my white colleagues would feel more comfortable, and I would be in a better position to achieve the success I was going after. I thought my race and gender would become a non-issue if I could somehow neutralize my blackness to make my coworkers feel comfortable.

But God always has a different plan, and let's just say things didn't work out the way I thought they would.

After a year at that job, the head of my department took me aside and told me that my work wasn't up to their standards and that I didn't have what it took to be a lawyer at their firm. Though I wasn't fired, per se, I knew he was definitely suggesting that I start looking for work elsewhere, particularly in the next three months. In law firms, this is what they call "pushing you out." No one is going to call security and tell you to leave the building immediately unless you do something crazy, but they will give you the "it's not a good fit; we suggest you start looking" speech.

I was crushed and completely devastated, to say the least. Yes, I made my fair share of mistakes as a first year, but I was willing to work hard and learn from them. On top of that, I had just bought a new condo in downtown Chicago, one that my dad told me not to buy. In hindsight, and after seeing many of my girlfriends go through the same exact thing, I realized that women of color don't often get the same level of mentoring, coaching, and sponsorship that others do in the workplace, and especially in corporate America. Our mistakes, however, are often magnified, while our colleagues often get the benefit of the doubt along with second, third, and fourth chances. For a black girl working in Big Law, a misplaced comma, a typo, or a late filing could be fatal and spell the end of her legal future at a firm. In contrast, the same mistake, if made by Tom or Steve may simply come with a "you need to pay closer attention next time."

I was young and completely new to this. Without anyone to confide in other than my father, I felt like a complete and total failure. Even worse, I felt ashamed that I had gone out of my way to be the kind of black girl they wanted me to be in order to fit their definition of success. I was out there working eighty hours a week, wearing this hot, uncomfortable wig, button-down shirts, V-neck sweaters from Ann Taylor, and pearl earrings with a matching pearl necklace. And for what? To be told I wasn't good enough.

My experience is all too common for black women working in corporate America. We often work hard, give our best, sacrifice our identity, adopt that high-pitched, nasally-sounding voice (that I hate), and it doesn't matter because more often than not, those in power prefer to support, mentor, and elevate their own even when they are less qualified. A few of us make it, but not as many as should, given the pool of over-talented, brilliant black women that I know personally who have been passed over time and time again for someone less than average.

But I digress. I left that law firm and was blessed to find another job at a new place called Jenner & Block. I say blessed because back then it was frowned upon to be a job hopper. Most lawyers would stay at a top firm for five or six years before they moved on, but here I was leaving my first firm after a mere eighteen months. It wasn't unheard of, but it was definitely unusual. I considered myself lucky to get a job at another top law firm in the city of Chicago doing complex work. I made a promise to myself that I would go in as the best version of myself and never deny who I was as a black woman. I wouldn't moderate my blackness or soften my personality in order to be successful on someone else's terms. I wanted to feel like I could come to the office with hair that grew from my own head and still feel confident, professional, and polished. This internal transformation ultimately became the seed for me writing the book *Thank God I'm Natural: The Ultimate Guide to Caring for and Maintaining Natural Hair.*

AN UNFAIR COMPROMISE

I've always been in love with anything and everything hair. Even as a young girl, I grew up playing in my grandma's beauty cabinet—doing my hair, washing it, blowing it dry. I'd use her Mrs. Cool, Sta-Sof-Fro, Care Free Curl, Blue Magic, or whatever she had on hand. I fell in love with the colors, scents, textures, and the way it transformed my look. I'd spend hours in the bathroom making a mess of my hair, washing and styling it again and again. It brought me so much joy.

Like most young black girls, I grew up with the idea that there was "good" hair and "bad" hair. It starts super early in most black families when a family member swoons over your cousin with the long Indian hair. I, on the other hand, had "difficult" to manage hair, and no one seemed to give a damn about it. So as I grew up, I just knew that my hair in its natural state was something to be ashamed of. My mom never said I had bad hair, but she started chemically straightening my hair at a very young age with the hope of making it easier to manage. We know today that this sends a message to our young girls to believe what society has always told them: that long, straight hair is good, and kinky hair, at any length, is bad.

When I saw the impact that my hair had on my professional life, I decided I wanted to do something about it, at least for myself. Through high school, I always had a fresh relaxer to make sure my edges were laid and my hair was healthy and flowing. Even when I set off to college, I took as much hair stuff as I could for my dorm. I had my own hooded hair dryer, a Marcel curling iron with a hot stove, a blow dryer with an attachment on the end, and products for days. People often asked if I was going to school to be a lawyer or a cosmetologist.

Keep in mind, like most black women, I straightened my kinky, curly hair using a chemical relaxer for the majority of my life in order to be seen as beautiful and to make my hair more manageable. The process of chemically straightening kinky hair seemed to do more damage than good. It was not only expensive, long, and painful, but it left many women with both physical and emotional scars. From a physical standpoint, it was common for women to experience traction alopecia, bald spots, and breakage, as well as extensive scalp burns from applying a lye-based product or sodium hydroxide in close proximity to the skin. From an emotional standpoint, black women were made to feel like they were not beautiful in their natural state because of society's subconscious messaging that put European beauty standards in the forefront. I often felt like I had to do everything in my power to succumb to this vicious cycle of chemically treating my hair in order to keep up with this misguided belief. After time, though, I found myself longing for a way to repair my hair from this damage and accept it in all of its kinky, curly glory.

It wasn't until I entered law school that I started to embrace my natural hair. I kept wearing my hair straight, but I stopped chemically treating it when I realized that going natural made my hair grow longer and healthier. I transitioned by wearing braids. However, when I took my braids down, I made the mistake of doing it in the shower without fully detangling first. It turned into a bird's nest, which meant I had to cut off all my hair just two months shy of starting my first law firm job. All I had left was a TWA.

Generally speaking, corporate America in the nineties was not too accepting of ethnic hairstyles, so in my mind, braids, faux locks, and crochet hairstyles were out of the question. My only real option back then was to wear a wig. Although this was absolutely not what I wanted to resort to in terms of hair, I buckled down and did what I thought I had to. But this experience left a bad taste in my mouth, and I was told I didn't belong in that environment anyway. I regrettably conceded to white comfort and reached an unspoken, unfair compromise with myself.

When I took stock of what happened at my first law firm, I realized that I should have showed up as the unapologetic, smart black woman that I am. Coming to work feeling like I had to be something I wasn't definitely had an impact on my work. In addition to having to do challenging work in corporate America, I had to deal with the subconscious belief that I was inferior or had to over-compensate by working twice as hard, because somehow being black made me less than. Again, all of this while wearing this hot, uncomfortable wig.

I realized that focusing on my appearance and blackness in the workplace was a distraction and prevented me from doing my best. My peers, however, were able to come to work as their authentic selves in an environment where they were comfortable. Once I removed that barrier and put my best foot forward, I saw a tremendous difference in my professional career and people's perception of me and my capabilities. I was done apologizing for my blackness in order to make others feel comfortable working with me. I vowed to focus on my work and become successful on my own terms, which ultimately meant working for myself. I knew this would be no easy feat. I would have to find a way to stack enough cash to leave my good-paying job and convince my dad to support my decision. But I was a go-getter, and there was simply no other option than to make my dreams a reality.

Chapter Five

DREAMING BIG

Fifteen years ago, the hair care shopping experience for black women was radically different from what it is today. Women often made their way over to the dusty shelves in the ethnic aisle of the local drugstore, where they would pick up a box of relaxer, hair lotion, and styling gel, and be on their way. Despite the fact that the ingredients were somewhat suspect and their performance was mediocre at best, women never questioned what they were buying.

When Carol's Daughter came on the scene in the late 1990s, it was a huge deal. Lisa Price, the founder, challenged what was considered mainstream hair care products and went from selling her natural products at parks and local festivals to having major real estate inside of Macy's stores, as well as a feature on the *Oprah Winfrey Show*. To top it off, she secured the investment of Will

Smith and Jada Pinkett and had celebrities like Mary J. Blige and Cassie swooning over her creations. A generation of young black women like myself were inspired.

Despite her success, the barriers to entry in the black hair care industry were still very prevalent. Contract fillers would require minimum runs of 50,000 units, and advertising in magazines and television was so expensive that it was cost prohibitive for a startup. Though we saw Lisa Price rise to the top, realistically, it didn't seem like something a little black girl from Detroit could duplicate without a background in chemistry or an outside investment of a million dollars.

Then came what was known as the browning of America. By 2003, Latinos were well on their way to becoming the majority in states like California, Texas, Arizona, Nevada, and Florida. Around the same time, artists like Jay-Z, Beyoncé, 50 Cent, Nelly, and Ludacris were gaining mainstream popularity and taking over the airwaves. But the biggest part of the movement took seed in the White House.

Around the same time, a young kid by the named of Mark Zuckerberg dropped out of Harvard as a sophomore and publicly launched a platform that we all know today as Facebook. When it first launched in 2003, only students with a Harvard email address had access to participate.

I remember logging on and it being super simple. Everyone had a page with some pictures of themselves, and it became an easy way to see what your friends on other parts of campus were up to. It quickly gained momentum and started to pick up steam, spreading like wildfire across our nation's college campuses, going from Harvard to Stanford to Yale. By 2008, the "like" button had been introduced, and this Facebook thing was now being used by the masses. This was before Facebook developed any type of advertising strategy and when pretty much all the content that appeared in your feed was organic.

In 2005, another company called YouTube came on the scene. In its infancy, YouTube was a place where amateurs could go and create their own content about whatever or record the happenings and upload it to a server to be shared with the world for all to see. Cultures of every shape and color became accessible and voiced across the internet.

In 2008, Barack Obama beat John McCain in what many considered to be an unexpected victory, even though black people came out in droves to vote for what could potentially be America's first black president. Many individuals waited hours to cast their vote, and though many people didn't believe something like this could happen, the support for him was endless. When Barack won, black people lost their minds. It was like the dawning of a new day. A veil had been lifted. People—myself included—were thinking that nothing was impossible, for the first time.

The excitement of having a black president, a black first lady, and two little black girls living in the White House was short-lived, but the pride and lasting effects that came with witnessing Barack Obama hold the highest office in the country is something that stands with me to this day. Barack's unapologetic entrance into a historically all-white space sparked something within me that made it almost impossible for me to give up on my dream of making a name for myself in this world.

While I was just starting to learn about the new technology that was surging in the marketplace, like Facebook and YouTube, I began to write *Thank God I'm Natural*. When I first went natural in 2002, I had a million questions and, frankly, nowhere to turn for answers. At times, I felt extremely discouraged and overwhelmed by the lack of information at my disposal, but what started out as a simple quest for answers became a full-blown passion of mine. I met and talked with hundreds of women from all walks of life, and although reasons for going natural vary, women with kinky hair were fed up with the breakage and damage caused by relaxers. We were tired of watching our hairlines disappear, while trying to hide our bald spots under wigs, weaves, and extensions. Like them, I was done being a slave to my hair and chemical relaxers. I was done with letting my tresses limit my life and enjoyment, whether that meant spending six hours in a beauty shop on a Saturday, running from rain drops, avoiding the swimming pool on vacation, or telling my man, "Not tonight, I just got my hair done."

The more I began to fall in love with and accept my natural hair, the more my confidence in my appearance grew. I began to realize that in the past, the only thing truly preventing me from being happy and fulfilling every aspect of my dream was merely my conception of myself. Once I realized that I didn't need to keep buying into the unhealthy and consuming expectation of a "perfect" appearance, I began to thrive.

Much to my surprise, my new hairstyle was also beginning to have a major influence on others in my life. After witnessing my transformation physically, professionally, and personally, many of my closest friends and colleagues made the decision to give up their relaxers and go natural. It was an amazing feeling to be the only natural woman in the room at times. Men often walked up to me and said, *"I love your hair,"* *"Damn, you're looking fine,"* or *"Can I touch your puff?"* Finally, after so many years, I had come to terms with my kinky tresses. Of course, everything I previously believed was nonsense; I never needed a wig in the first place to be accepted at my job or to be considered attractive. I just had to be myself and learn to accept my own natural hair for what it was: a beautiful and real reflection of who I am as a person and as a black woman.

The idea for *Thank God I'm Natural* came after my wig-wearing experience at my first job. I wanted to move forward and document my experience as a black woman working in corporate America with natural hair and also give other women the information they needed to go natural. Back then, the internet was in its infancy, and Google was a mere five years old. There were a few blogs here and there for women who were interested in going natural, as well as a website called nappturality.com, where I would spend hours in chat rooms and forums learning about how to take care of my hair. It was an underground community that I was proud to be a part of.

I thought the online message boards were a great place for information, but a minority of the posters were what we called "Natural Nazis." These were the women who were like the Supreme Court Justice Antonin Scalia of the natural hair community; they had a very strict and conservative interpretation of what it meant to be natural. These women would go in on innocent users who would ask very basic questions related to straightening their natural hair or coloring their hair for variety. For them, natural hair meant no heat, no chemicals, no nothing. They were totally on the juices and berries train, and

I saluted them, but for some of us, that wasn't going to get it. Many women need products in order to make a seamless transition.

Sadly, there were very few products commercially available for women who were looking to embrace this lifestyle. You couldn't just walk into a major retailer and pick up a jar of Honey Miracle Hair Mask like you can now. To make matters worse, very few, if any, black women owned companies that were manufacturing products for this demographic. Still, there was a demand for more natural products specifically formulated for textured hair. While I had a personal need for products, I never expected to go out and change the world or help create an industry based on my own personal problems. It was never a means to get rich, but rather to give women the information they needed to transition out of their relaxer, beyond what was available on hair care message boards. *Thank God I'm Natural* took me nearly three years to write because back in 2006, there was tons of information to sift through. After doing extensive research and organizing the information I came across, what originally began as a small pamphlet ended up as a 300-page book.

I initially questioned my ability to write on this subject. All I could think about was how I failed the written placement test my freshman year at Harvard and how I had to take Expository 10, the remedial writing class. That setback stuck with me for a long time and caused me to doubt what I was capable of. While I had always been good at math, science, and oral communication, writing was my Achilles' heel. Likewise, I was a lawyer, not a cosmetologist. Who was I to be giving anyone advice on caring for their natural hair when I was so new to this experience myself? But I kept at it, hired a coach, did my research, put my heart into it, and realized that I needed to trust in a higher power greater than myself. I could have focused on what I didn't have or what I didn't know, but I made the choice to keep moving forward.

When I was working at Jenner, I would get to work every day at 7 a.m. to write. Every week, I put in about seventy hours at the office and worked four to five hours every Saturday morning at the coffee shop. When I received a call with an opportunity to work at Oracle, which was a nine-to-five job in downtown Chicago, I took a major pay cut and stepped off the lawyer path to work on my passion while also paying the bills. Looking back on that time, I have no clue how I was able to juggle getting my company off the ground while working at my day job. It had to be God. When I left Jenner, I promised myself that Oracle would be the last job where I worked for someone else.

As I was working on the book, I started to see a handful of natural hair care brands take off and gain national distribution in places like Target. I looked at their success and felt like I was falling behind. I really wanted to work on my products, but my intuition and God's voice told me to focus on writing the book. I believed that it would set me apart as an expert and help me cultivate a following to ensure that my company had staying power as a brand. Maybe He was preparing me for this current project without me even knowing. In hindsight, it was one of the best choices I've ever made.

In July of 2009, after many long and tireless hours of writing, I dropped *Thank God I'm Natural: The Ultimate Guide to Caring for and Maintaining Natural Hair*, not thinking it would ever be this hit bestseller or develop a cult following. I ordered a thousand books, and when they showed up on my doorstep, my dad said, "Who are you going to sell these books to? If you can't get rid of these books in six months, you need to give them away." It was a perfect storm. In October, almost three months after the books arrived, the Chris Rock movie *Good Hair* hit theaters nationwide, sparking a major conversation about hair, relaxers, and beauty in the black community. I sold out of my book less than one month after the movie was released. The response was amazing, and the timing couldn't have been more perfect. As they say in the South, it was like catching lighting in a bottle.

Because of the provocative nature of the film, newspapers were writing left and right about the movie and were looking for "experts" to give their opinions on the movie and why black women were hooked on relaxers, AKA the creamy crack. Somehow, thanks to social media, people learned about my book, which resulted in it being featured in *Essence*, *Black Enterprise*, *USA Today*, you name it.

After seeing *Good Hair*, women were going natural in droves. Black women were, for the first time since the Afro was popular in the seventies, starting to consider going back to their natural roots. What was once viewed as a style for the political, woke, or militant was now being embraced by the masses. Still, for the most part, many women didn't know what they were doing because they had been chemically straightening their hair for so long, often from a very young age. In turn, many black women, including a few of the bloggers and YouTubers who were just starting to launch their brands, turned to my book for guidance.

The book touched women of all ages. It was a total movement. Men were buying the book as gifts for their wives and sisters. Women were buying it for their daughters as a way of saying, "Stay natural. You are beautiful just the way you are." Our world was changing. All over the internet, women were chronicling their hair journeys on blogs and on YouTube. Women like Chary Jay and NikkiMae were in their bathrooms in all of their natural glory, no makeup and no filter, having honest conversations with their followers about their hair, their lifestyle, and their fears on this journey. This was before the ring lights, filters, and movie-quality sets that we see bloggers using today.

People were skyrocketing to celebrity-dom for showing women the many different hairstyles they created, while offering their authentic and honest opinion on what products were best for twist-outs or flat twists. People highlighted their natural transitions and the emotional rollercoasters that came along with the journey.

Every time a news anchor took off her wig and came on the air with her natural curls, it was a conversation piece. Every time a major company put a black woman on television promoting their products with curly or natural hair, it was a big deal. It stirred up so much conversation, like when Tyra Banks was the first black woman to grace the cover of *Sports Illustrated* in the 1990s, and people damn near lost their mind. Even though our hair was for us and by us, seeing ourselves represented in the media with big halos of curls was incredibly self-affirming.

Women with kinks, curls, and waves often lived with doubts of whether they could find love, get the job if they interviewed with natural hair, or handle the amount of work that came with maintaining these styles. Black women started to celebrate and talk about the power of black beauty, instead of hoping to emulate a white aesthetic. There was a larger conversation going on about why and how black women had reached a point where they weren't able to be their true and authentic selves. It was beautiful yet utter pandemonium.

At the same time, Facebook and Twitter made it so companies could share information and tips on caring for natural hair in a way that was very organic. As a result, black women's search for information on how to embrace this lifestyle choice was now at their fingertips. It was easier than ever before to have a conversation about the things they cared about—their hair, bodies, diets, etc. Everything was on the table. Social media was a total whirlwind, and everyone, including myself, was learning what this new level of connectedness could bring.

The availability of my book gave me a major opportunity to be a part of this conversation. I traveled across the world, to places as far as South Africa, to different shows and meetups to talk about this issue of hair, beauty, and identity and how they were interwoven. It was a time unlike any other, and the beauty of it was that black female business owners were able to capitalize on this trend and build successful brands, many of which you see on the shelves today.

For so long, kinky hair was something to be controlled, tamed, or managed. Now, women were given a blank canvas, and every inch was used to create more intricate and varied styles than we had in the past forty years. While the Afro, in all of its uniformity, gained tremendous popularity in the 1970s, by 2010, black women were experimenting with natural hair, creating everything from rod sets to Bantu knots to twist-outs and more, to celebrate their crowns.

I met women who would cry when they shared their story of going natural and doing the Big Chop. There were also those who were scared to make the move for fear of losing their job, or in some instances, their husband. It was a movement that took me to hair shows, libraries, bookstores, churches, and festivals, where I spread the gospel of "loving yourself just the way you are." Being a part of their support system felt so natural, no pun intended. It almost felt like breathing. I started to realize that this was what I was called to do.

In addition to selling books, I was now also selling branded apparel with the words "Thank God I'm Natural" and a silhouette of a black woman with a hoop earring. It was classy; it was sophisticated; it was tgin. Those years were crazy yet rewarding; we sold a ton of books and even more t-shirts with the hope of conveying just how beautiful black women were.

With the success of the book, it became clear that there

was a demand for more. People were appreciative of the information but were starting to wonder where the products were. After spending three years traveling, promoting the book, and selling apparel, I wanted to begin focusing on my products, but I was scared. I was a lawyer, not a chemist. I had no real background in science, and I was no Carol's Daughter when it came to knowing my way around the kitchen. I also didn't possess a cosmetology degree, but I was setting out to create products better than those that were currently on the shelf in major retailers.

It didn't add up from a conventional standpoint, but I kept my focus and remained prayerful that if this was my assignment, God would supply everything I needed to complete it. I had no choice but to step out in faith and start mixing things in my kitchen and try to use some of the shampoo and conditioner recipes I came across in various natural beauty books. These products provided me with my training wheels for formulation. Still, my creations were not shelf stable, and I knew I needed a chemist to really make this thing pop. I tried googling ethnic hair chemists but really didn't make much progress. Back then, people's websites were super basic and didn't give a real sense of their capabilities. So instead, I took a chance and started asking people who worked in the industry for their recommendations.

Luckily, Chicago is home to many Johnson Products and

Soft Sheen employees, so I worked my connections to get a few leads toward finding a manufacturer who was willing to deal with a rookie like myself. The opportunity came when I was at a trade show one day. The young guy in the booth next to us worked for a major company, and I shyly asked him if he could make our products. He told me he wouldn't be able to make them, but he gave me the name of someone who could.

That was just the break I needed. After getting in touch with the chemist and factory that he recommended, I worked for almost two years on developing our Butter Cream Daily Moisturizer and our Twist & Define Cream. It was a scary time for me. I knew nothing other than my kitchen recipes. I didn't know anything about the hair industry, so instead of using the chemist for all five products, which would have been a hefty investment, I decided to perfect my skills and develop our shampoo, conditioner, and best-selling Honey Miracle Hair Mask on my own to save money in case the entire venture was a flop.

The products had to be good, though. This was the new age of social media and online reviews, and performance was everything. There were no second chances, so I gave it my all and spent the time to really get it right. I could have rushed and just put anything out there, but the stakes were too high, and that wasn't my style anyway.

Despite all the positivity that came with black women embracing their natural tresses during this movement, there was still a tremendous amount of division that exists to this day around hair typing. Silky, shiny, and elongated ringlets were considered by some to be better than short, tight, kinky hair, which I happen to possess. It was plain as day in many of the advertisements that featured women with loose curls that promised longer, silkier hair or more "curl definition."

Although people profited handsomely from this kind of messaging, it left a lot of women disappointed and feeling like this natural hair thing was only for women with a certain curl pattern. I saw an opportunity when developing my products and decided to keep things simple and focus merely on healthy hair. Not long hair. Not shiny hair. Not silky hair. Just healthy hair. Hair that was soft, moisturized, and manageable. This message and promise resonated with women of all hair types and textures, especially women with kinkier hair types. It's a mission we, at tgin, continue to work toward to this day. Over the next few years, I worked diligently to formulate products that delivered on their promises.

The day our products were finally done was one of the happiest moments in my career. I felt pride like a mother who had just given birth. After so much work, the day had finally come—I had my own products. Using what I learned from selling my books and t-shirts, I started getting the word out and sending samples to every blogger I knew who had shown me love over the years or whom I had built relationships with at different natural hair meetups. We went hard when it came to marketing and sent out super slick mailer boxes full of products, which have become industry standard today. Bloggers would open their boxes and post pictures on Instagram, and their followers would come straight to our website to purchase the products.

Around the same time, Miss Jessie's, Shea Moisture, and several other brands were launching in Target. This was huge. I looked on with admiration, but I personally felt like the door was closing just as I was getting started. It's that same feeling you get when you see your girlfriend getting married, having a baby, buying a house, getting a divorce, and doing it again before you even get engaged once. It's not right, but that's how it felt.

Despite making so much progress, I was still very much afraid. I had major doubts about my ability to come in and create products for other women when I had no background in this industry, and the only chemistry class I had ever taken was in high school. Still, I was able to do it. I didn't know much then, and there's still a lot I don't know today, but, when it came to getting from point A to point B, I realized I had to put one foot in front of the other, ask people for help, believe in myself, and just go for it.

The fear of feeling like an impostor or not knowing what to do, in many instances, held me back. I have learned from personal experience I can be my own worst enemy. With self-sabotaging thoughts and negative mindsets lowering my aspirations, I considered abandoning my hopes and dreams, both personally and professionally, a thousand times. I've wrestled with voices that tell me I'm not worthy or deserving of more, or that I'm not enough. I had to understand that my fears were not my reality. Instead, I must face these fears head-on in order to be successful.

Women often asked me for advice on how to start their own businesses and how to get over the fear and self-doubt that come with taking the risk. I always tell them that despite all that I have accomplished, I'm still scared of success, scared of dreaming big, scared of wanting more for my company, scared of going to the next level, scared of trying something different and failing at it. But if we truly have faith, we must trust that God will give us the desires of our heart and equip us with all the right tools should certain opportunities present themselves.

If you're reading this book for a bit of inspiration, ask yourself what you've been holding yourself back from doing. What dreams are you not chasing? What opportunities are you not seeking because you feel you're not enough, not prepared, not ready, or not experienced? Remember, you have everything you need within. Tap into your gift and take a leap of faith.

.

Chapter Six

UNDER PRESSURE

Over the years, I've come to realize that starting a company is a lot like making a diamond. Diamonds are made from four things: carbon, heat, time, and a lot of pressure. Dreams start off as carbon, and it takes heat, time, and a lot of pressure for it to transform from a lump of coal into a diamond.

The same can be said for relationships, business, etc. It takes a certain amount of time and pressure to work through and become successful. In my case, it took ten long years to build tgin and to get to the point where my eyes were opened to see areas I needed to work on personally. Sometimes it will take even longer before you're able to see your diamond. Other times, it's not about the diamond itself, but what you learn about yourself during the process that's most valuable.

Ask yourself what your diamond is—what is your end goal? Whatever that end goal is, stay disciplined, but remember to be kind to yourself, nurture your personal relationships, and enjoy the journey along the way.

As I built my company, pressure was always present. It was a constant hum in the back of my mind every single day. In hindsight, I realize that I wouldn't be where I am today without that pressure, not just in business but in personal relationships. I've had to face tests in my friendships and with family-related matters. When we think of diamonds, we think of money and fame. Sometimes that's true, but sometimes that pressure creates good character, good judgment, good decision-making, and even insight and self-awareness.

Deep down, I always knew tgin would be something big. In my head, it already was. I was chasing something bigger than me. But when I look back on where I started and where I am today, it's difficult to imagine that I've been able to accomplish this much. When I walk into our factory and see the shelves filled with products and people working on machinery and equipment, I think back to when my baby was just a tiny little lump of coal, nothing more than a dream. There was a time when I was literally selling products out of the trunk of my car. That's where my journey began; that was the coal that grew to become my diamond.

Back when I graduated from law school, people seemed so committed to a singular, linear trajectory and defining their success on traditional terms, like making partner at a law firm. But today, I find more and more lawyers who are working full-time and doing something they're passionate about. They might have a baking business or do makeup for extra cash, or they might even be writing screenplays. People want to feel more in control of their destiny while having a creative outlet, which is to be applauded.

As tgin was starting to take off, this was not the case, and people had a much different view toward entrepreneurship. After leaving Jenner, I started working at Oracle because of the tremendous amount of flexibility it provided. There was a time when working for a corporate legal department in-house was not viewed as being as prestigious as working for a law firm. In-house was a place where people went when they couldn't make partner at a law firm. That view has completely changed over the years, and now in-house jobs are viewed as being just as challenging, if not more complicated, than working for a law firm. When I went in-house, I took such a huge risk because having a nine-to-five job with work-from-home privileges would provide me with greater flexibility to focus on my little company.

Unfortunately, entrepreneurship was brutal. Instead of going into an office every Saturday and Sunday and working on legal briefs, memorandums, and exhibits, I was literally in a black tgin shirt and black shorts in parks and farmers' markets around the city of Chicago selling shampoo and shea butter. I worked every weekend, whether I was at a festival, a hair show, working on the books, or responding to emails. I traveled all the time, and to this day, travel is hard for me. We have to go out there and "shake hands and kiss babies" to tell people about our products. Even when you don't have the marketing budget that larger companies like L'Oréal and Unilever have, you do have the ability to connect with people on a personal level. I've learned that building these relationships is extremely important for any small business that focuses on consumer products.

To say my friends were a little skeptical and somewhat confused by my choices would be an understatement. Over time, however, as we started to gain traction, I could see them coming around to the idea that this tgin thing may have some legs. As far as my dad, he believed in me since the very beginning. Along the way, I think he struggled a bit to accept that he and my mom sacrificed so much to send their daughter to Harvard Law School, and now she wanted to be in the beauty industry. While he may never have imagined the company would be what it is today, he has always maintained a healthy dose of realism, which came in handy and supported me throughout the entire journey.

My success was inevitable. You see, the beauty industry is made for hustlers like me. In Detroit, a beautician or stylist can take home well over $100K in a year without ever earning a college degree. Although this was and is still considered a pretty penny, beauticians are somewhat notorious for making a lot of money and spending a lot of money, as well. Things like health insurance, 401(k)s, and retirement plans are not necessarily top of mind, but they are necessary expenses that come with the territory of being self-employed. While being a beautician is a totally respectable profession, it doesn't have the same ring that comes with being a Harvard-trained lawyer. Still, I knew this was the path for me and that I could make an honest living doing what I loved.

It's messed up, though, because most beauticians are women, but the people that profit the most from this industry are men who are either company owners or major decision-makers and CEOs at multi-national corporations. If I was going to go into the beauty business, with my education and credentials, people would expect me to work for a company like L'Oréal, Unilever, or Procter & Gamble. But again, I wasn't living my life for anyone but myself, and so like many beauticians, I opted to stand on my own feet and make a living selling hair care products and talking to women about their problems, whether hair-related or personal.

In the process of chasing my dream, I encountered my fair share of haters and naysayers. There were the times when I would be out at the African Fest, in between the woman selling body wraps and the lady selling body oils, and my colleagues from the legal profession would stop by our table with this little smirk on their face, like, "Oh, what are you doing?" To this day, I still remember all the looks and comments. There were those lawyers who looked down on me and said in a condescending tone, "Oh, that little thing you're doing? How cute." Other people would ask me why I wasn't giving my legal career my all or why I wasn't focused on becoming general counsel.

For me, it all came down to focus. I could've let the naysayers get into my head, but I had a plan for myself and a vision for this company. I know some people would have liked to defend themselves in that situation, but I'm not really that type. I learned my lesson early on while working in corporate America; if I was going to work hard and invest in something 120 percent, I felt the greatest ROI (return on investment) would come from working for myself.

Despite my focus, my lawyer friends continued to question my career path, and I saw people lap me, making double what I was making when I left Oracle because they continued to climb. I refused to get discouraged when my friends were buying BMWs and Mercedes and fur coats while I was still driving my Ford Escape truck from law school. The same was true when they were moving into big homes or taking fancy vacations while I was still living a fairly conservative lifestyle, one I still maintain to this day because of the sacrifice it takes to grow a company and hire and invest in top-shelf talent.

To add insult to injury, I remember dating successful businessmen or executives who would tell me that whatever I was working on was never going to be bigger than what he could accomplish, so it was probably best if I focused on his dreams and pushed mine to the side. Then there were the guys who would date me and were super attentive when they thought I sold shea butter and t-shirts for a living, and then would ghost me when they found out I also had a "real job" as a lawyer at a Fortune 100 company.

Despite all of the detractors and distractions, I had to run my own race. I had to keep going. I was on a highly unusual path, but it was my passion. To stay focused, I had to tune all of that out and never let people get me off my square. They couldn't see what I could see. They couldn't see this big dream that I had inside of me, the dream that kept me up at night and woke me up early in the morning, that caused me to work every weekend in a coffee shop, that had me on my feet every Saturday talking to women about their hair, that took me all over the country. It didn't hurt that people looked down on me. I knew the day would come when they would see. It was all one major sacrifice, and my own motivation fueled me to get through it. This was something I was going to do, and no one was going to stop me.

What did sting was the harshness and discrimination of the business world in general. Despite having great ideas, black women have a much harder time getting funding, purely because of the color of their skin or their gender. I have seen young white men blow through millions of dollars to start companies that later fail, only to have people sign up to take the ride with them all over again because they've learned some great lessons. In other communities, you can look to Mark Zuckerberg, Bill Gates, Steve Jobs, and others who dropped out of college to go chase their dreams. As a black woman raised by two black parents who hadn't come from much, that wasn't an option for me. I couldn't drop out of school or leave law to nurture and grow this company. My dad couldn't write me a check for half-a-million dollars of seed money for my hair-brained idea. Some people are able to start eight, nine, or ten businesses before the eleventh one finally takes off. That wasn't my situation. I had one shot.

Entrepreneurship is a scary journey, particularly when you have no financial backing, have put your entire life savings on the line, and have to work two jobs for something you believe in that no one else can see. People often say you have to be crazy to start a company, and it's absolutely true. It takes a certain level of focus—and I mean *laser* focus—determination, and a little bit of crazy to pursue entrepreneurship. A great idea is never enough. It really comes down to execution and the ability to withstand the pressure and storms that come with the territory. Sacrifices have to be made, and your business must become your spouse, mother, best friend, teacher, and lover. For so long, tgin was my everything, and I was everything for tgin.

When you're first starting out, you will have to wear many hats. You'll have to be operations, marketing and social media, administration, payroll, bookkeeping, product development, shipping, logistics, and whatever else needs to be done. I tell people at tgin that I've done literally every job there is. I've made product, put labels on packaging, ran customer service (hell, customers somehow still call me to this day, and I have no idea how they got my number), posted to social media, paid invoices, submitted payroll, reviewed contracts, swept and mopped floors, and cleaned out the refrigerator. Seeing how each job is done has given me a full appreciation for what it takes for each person on my team to be successful. This wasn't what I set out to do intentionally, but with no real financial safety net, I had no other choice.

Like I said, sacrifices must be made—both physically and financially. When the company was first getting off the ground after our products launched, we were working out of my two-bedroom, twelve-hundred-square-foot condo, packing and shipping boxes. For nearly a year and a half, my home looked like a small factory. We were cramped like sardines, but we were shipping and pushing product out the door like clockwork. There were oils, bottles, and boxes everywhere. I had all kinds of people in my home helping me make and ship products and just get everything off the ground. You would walk in my apartment and get hit in the face with the smell of patchouli. Even worse, over time, everything in my refrigerator started to taste like sugar pear shea butter because we would often have to refrigerate product in order for it to turn solid.

In hindsight, running a business out of my apartment wasn't the safest or smartest idea, but financially, I had no choice. I was scared to invest in a commercial space because I was afraid of signing a lease. I didn't want to ruin my credit if the company suddenly went belly-up. So, I hung on as long as I could until it became unbearable for myself and for the people working for me. It ultimately got to the point where I had no choice but to look for a space. We just couldn't function at that level anymore, and the mail lady was getting annoyed with having to pick up hundreds of boxes at a time on a residential route.

After doing some research, I came across a startup incubator housed in a warehouse on the west side of Chicago, right outside of the Fulton-Kinzie Corridor. At the time, the building was filled to capacity, but at the interview, I convinced the landlord that having the space would allow me to put in the necessary work to get into Target. Note, Target had not even called us at this point, so I was just claiming it and breathing it into existence. Clearly, it worked.

Still, moving into a commercial space was a huge risk. I had to sign a lease, and was now responsible for not only payroll, but rent as well. Quitting my day job at Oracle wasn't really an option. Although tgin was just starting to take off and make a little money, I always had to put money back into the company in order to support its growth, whether this meant hiring more people, investing in inventory, or dedicating resources to marketing. As a result, I wasn't taking a salary, and I had no choice but to juggle my day job and side hustle in order to pay my mortgage and car note. tgin was making just enough money to cover payroll.

Although most of my memories as senior corporate counsel were fond, Oracle was a very demanding place. It was a literal shark tank. The company was very bottom-line driven and expected a degree of professionalism and output from its legal team. They had no problem letting go of anyone who didn't make their numbers two quarters in a row. As such, the teams I supported were always on pins and needles to hit their sales plan. If they didn't, they could be out in the cold with a mortgage to pay and a family to support. The company also didn't foster a stable work-life balance. People often made very good money there but could get calls at all times of the day. I was working multiple time zones from the office in Chicago, servicing people who lived on the West Coast, in the Central region, in London, and in India.

My work was very good for me as an attorney and allowed me to develop a confidence in my abilities that would have taken me years to gain in a firm. Firms have several layers of management; an employee often reviews two to three people's work, and in turn, two to three seniors above them are reviewing their work, unless they are a senior partner. But at Oracle, I was given two days of training, a legal manual, and then a "good luck"—I was off to the races. I loved it. I was twenty-six years old, making legal decisions and giving advice on deals valued in the millions. The people who hired me trusted me and believed in my legal ability.

At Oracle, my managers tended to be very hands off, and no news from them was good news. However, if they somehow got a complaint about your work, your responsiveness, or your accuracy from one of the teams you supported, it was a major red flag. I brought this same spirit of trust and self-management to my own company, which has been both a good thing and a bad thing.

If something rises to my level, be it a mistake or a personality conflict, it's usually a cause for concern. Given that I was stretched so thin during those startup months, it was imperative that I hired people I could trust to get the job done without me having to look over their shoulder; I needed people who could handle the freedom that came with this level of flexibility. When young people come to work for me, they are often shocked by how much responsibility and autonomy they have, because they are so used to working for micro-managers. It was a hard line to toe, and we're still improving upon this today, but my mantra was always, "I have faith in you," or "Figure it out."

Juggling two jobs that both required 100 percent of me was stressful, to say the least. I had absolutely no idea how stressed I was until I finished my cancer treatments. I had known nothing but hard work all my life, and stress had become the silent hum in the background I was used to dealing with. Being a black woman working in corporate America added to the constant level of stress that comes with balancing two careers. It doesn't matter if a woman of color has earned twenty Harvard degrees, the Presidential Medal of Freedom, and a Nobel Prize in physics, she'll most likely always feel like people are judging her work not based on its quality, but based on their own prejudices.

The nice thing about Oracle was that I didn't feel like I constantly had to prove myself; I was working with people from around the world who had no real opportunity to meet with me in person. For the most part, 99.5 percent of the business I conducted was over the phone, which meant people had to go out of their way to find out I was black, unless I slipped up and let the "culture" come out, as that was known to happen at times.

Given that I negotiated the same five or six license agreements over and over for almost ten years, I was able to use that to my advantage. I got really, really good at my work, developed an expertise, and tried to keep to myself as much as possible. People enjoyed working with me; they knew that I knew my stuff, but there was this lingering curiosity—even internally, with my bosses—as to why I wasn't trying to climb the ladder. That just wasn't where I was headed. I knew I was destined for more, that I was capable of becoming my own boss and conducting my own business. Truth be told, I had no interest in working for someone else for much longer, so I worked my butt off to make sure I didn't have to.

* * *

They say it's lonely at the top, but it's also lonely in the middle and at the bottom when you're first starting out as an entrepreneur. As I built tgin, I often felt alone chasing a dream in my head and dealing with too many problems to burden my friends and family with. Even to this day, there are times I feel very much alone. I could easily fix this by picking up the phone to call one of my girlfriends for a brunch meetup or by going on a girlfriends' getaway, but sometimes, it's difficult to disconnect from a dream, so I sadly ended up living in isolation. To top it off, it can come across as insensitive when you make a habit of disappearing for long periods of time only to resurface and pull a "Do you wanna be friends again?" act when you're doing well. I know I'm guilty of this, and it's one of those things that I wish I did differently in the beginning of my business venture.

Whether you're winning or losing, you often feel like you're in this entrepreneur game all by yourself—just you and God. Especially if you're losing, it can feel like no one fully appreciates or understands the fears that come with having your own business and constantly doubting every move you make. I often wondered if I'd make enough to pay my employees or if my manufacturer would be able to deliver on schedule. It was an endless dance, an emotional rollercoaster that I was on all by myself. It's definitely not for everyone, and I was juggling it all with a full-time job. I needed a thick skin to be able to withstand the bad days along with the good.

When you're winning, people are often unable to relate, and you feel the need to downplay your accomplishments, especially if they are happening back to back. As a result, you draw inward and closer to the people on your team who know exactly what it took to get to this winning point. They, for better or worse, become your friends and, in some instances, your family.

My obsession with work had an impact on all of my female relationships; I was losing girlfriends left and right. Some of the relationships fell apart because of the company and some because of outside influences—a guy, or maybe how busy I was—but at that time, I just didn't have any room to step away from tgin. The sad thing was, I didn't care. If a girlfriend and I fell out for one reason or another, I often dreaded the thought of the "Let's have brunch and talk about our feelings" conversation, on so many levels. I've never been the girl to work through her feelings, hence the reason why I'm here. I also didn't feel like making time to work on those relationships, because it seemed like sitting down, listening to your concerns, and trying to come up with some artificial resolution would take time that I didn't have. I could have tried to make amends, but customers, retailers, paperwork, my employees, and the factory were always calling.

There was always pressure from people reaching out to tell me that I didn't answer when they called or that I missed a special occasion. It's true; I missed performances, and I didn't come over when people called me crying. I think about good girlfriends of mine getting married when I went out of town on business. I remember my closest friend being pregnant with her first child, and instead of being at her baby shower, I went to a trade show in South Africa. I tried to make up for it by helping with the planning and contributing financially, but at the end of the day, my work came first. I could pick and choose what I did, but I was in too deep. Do I regret it? In some instances, I do. I've had to learn from my mistakes and nurture the close relationships I have now in order to make better decisions.

But back then, there was no competition; tgin came first, and everyone knew it. I knew my friends were pulling away in some form or fashion. In turn, I found that in my major moments of crisis, those who had been my friends were not there to support me, and it hurt. My company was at a very unique place, and I felt like my baby and team needed me. I wouldn't be where I am today if I didn't make those choices. At the same time, though, making those choices helped me find out who my true friends were and what I needed to do to become a better friend myself.

The men I dated were no exception to this neglect. I

tended to attract those who weren't looking for anything serious because I, myself, was emotionally unavailable. These men would often prey on the fact that I could never fully engage. While I made time to go on dates, people knew that I wasn't a nine-to-five girl that they could cuddle up with on the couch to watch *Game of Thrones* every week. I was hyper-focused, and I attracted people who were also emotionally unavailable and saw me as an opportunity. They could make me girlfriend one of three; if I only gave 20 percent, they only had to give 20 percent. I think people could quickly see through what I was offering up, but I wasn't self-aware enough to realize that part of the problem was me and my unhealthy work-life balance.

In short, my friends, family, and the guys I dated became collateral damage to my success. I was hyper-focused on winning the race, selling however much I needed to sell, getting my products into Target stores, or helping my company become what I knew it could be. In the process, I left a trail of broken relationships that I never stopped to acknowledge. It was like getting a flat tire, leaving the car on the side of the road, then hopping into another vehicle because you're so focused on getting to your destination. I was committed to the race more than the journey, and I wasn't going to let anyone or anything stop me.

I even let my hobbies go. I remember being a part of a

women's tennis league, going to practices every Monday and playing in matches every weekend. It had been such a safe girl space, where we'd not only play but go out for drinks and hang out. It became another obstruction of my time, so I chose tgin. The same thing happened with Sunday night dinners and book club. I had to put all of that to the side. Until after I got cancer, everything was about the company.

I continued to press on with business like so many of us do when we have failed to deal with long-held trauma. Only now am I beginning to see just how strong my addiction to working was. We all have our vices—be it food, sex, liquor, drugs, bad relationships, or in my case, shampoo.

Part of the reason I'm writing this book is because people always like to celebrate what I have accomplished, but clearly, I'm successful because I'm dealing with something much bigger than the book you're reading. I left a trail of neglected people and unresolved situations because I was so committed to running this race, burying the pain of losing my mom and avoiding the trauma her death caused. I've learned that it's so important to nurture your relationships along the path to wherever you're going and deal with your issues, because they have a way of manifesting themselves in your mind, body, and spirit. In my case, the unresolved trauma of losing my mom in 1996 caused me to develop an addiction to work, which manifested itself into a cancer diagnosis twenty years later.

I urge those of you who are looking to start your own business or chase your dreams to put things in perspective and make clear decisions about your priorities. If you're serious about your dreams, you have to be focused and disciplined. You need to have a plan, but that plan should not push you into developing complete tunnel vision. It's also important to practice self-care and self-awareness. Find a way to balance that focus, that drive, and that intensity with relationships and the people you surround yourself with, the people you care about. People matter; they keep us grounded and help us relieve some of that stress. The hard work, for the most part, is non-negotiable.

Just remember, pressure comes with the territory. Becoming a better person should be a part of the journey, as well.

Chapter Seven

WHO CAN
I TRUST?

People sometimes see tgin on the cover of a magazine, in a major retail outlet, or on TV and think, "Wow, that happened fast." But trust me, we're a story almost fifteen years in the making. If I had waited for these big moments to define me, I would've quit a long time ago. The only way you make it from point A to point B, as an entrepreneur or in life, is to celebrate the small wins along the way. I found this to be true when it came to both running a company and beating cancer.

I knew from the time I was twenty-five that I wanted to have my own product line on the shelves, but oftentimes, my dream seemed to elude me. It always felt as if I was in a long, dark tunnel, and there wasn't even a glimmer of light. As a result, I had to do the hard work and grind day after day, but also take the time to celebrate the small wins and victories along the way. I figured that if I overly focused on the goal or result, I would always be living life from a place of lack instead of a place of abundance. I needed to channel my doubts into something positive and enriching for my company.

But the process of changing my mindset was anything but easy. I knew deep down that my company would eventually take off; I just didn't know how to ask for help and where I could turn to get it. I had to be patient, trust in God, and allow things to be revealed to me. Along the way, I set goals for myself but no deadlines. I would write my goals on small sheets of paper and tape them to a wall in my home office or put them on a notepad and tuck them away in a drawer. Seeing my goals often, in my own handwriting, was an ongoing reminder that I was working toward something. I never obsessed about a particular goal, but writing it down made a huge difference. This guidance is even found in the Bible when the Lord says to Habakkuk, "Write down the revelation and make it plain upon tables, that he may run that readeth it" (Hab. 2:2 KJV). Simply put, there is power in writing down your goals.

Too often, people lose their way in the pursuit of reaching their goals because they're so focused on landing the big contract or securing a big TV appearance. They fail to focus on the little things, like getting your papers incorporated, buying your website domain, finalizing the packaging design, or coming up with your name and slogan. All of these little pieces are critical for the success of any business and must be celebrated.

For me, building a website, coming up with product names, and developing our formulas may have seemed small at the time, but looking back on these moments, they were a huge deal, particularly for someone who had no background in the beauty industry. My biggest concern, even with all of these little successes, was my ability to find customers, but I didn't let it affect me. I just focused on having a good product and wrote down small goals that I could achieve within three to six months. Imagine my surprise when people actually decided to believe in what I was doing and hand over their hard-earned money for the items I was selling. To this day, I remember that the first person to buy my book on Amazon was a close friend of mine, Ebbie Parsons, who purchased the book for his wife Ayanna when she was thinking of going natural. This was back before we had products and were a long way from getting into Target. I knew that if I could sell one book, then I could sell a thousand more.

Our Facebook page was another avenue that shocked me with its success. I remember when we started with just one hundred fans, and our page gradually grew to 25,000 followers. This was a big deal for us. As our page continued to grow, I could see our messages starting to take off and resonate, whether people were posting the book or the t-shirts online or just joining our community with their support. I often saved positive emails and Facebook comments that people sent, and printed them out to continue to give me encouragement. Although I was a long way from getting on the shelves of major retailers, these small wins were monumental, and they still are.

* * *

As I was struggling to get tgin off the ground, everyone, especially those in Chicago, was starting to become obsessed with the cult of the startup. Small was becoming the new big. One of our neighboring companies in the Kinzie Corridor, Goose Island, or 312 Beer, became the leader in the craft beer movement. Their small brewery went from producing 150,000 barrels a year of their best-selling brews, such as 12, Honker's, and India Pale Ale, to being purchased for close to $40 million by Anheuser-Busch. They saw a problem in their industry—beer didn't have a lot of flavor or variety—and sought to fill that need. In the process, they created numerous jobs and brought a lot of publicity to the city of Chicago. They restored our faith in the idea that small guys could be in big business and highlighted the importance of small businesses in our local economy.

After selling our hair care products almost entirely online for over a year, we got our "Goose Island" break in July 2014, when our products launched in a local Mariano's store, a new chain of stores being built throughout the Chicagoland area. Mariano's garnered a lot of press and attention for creating an upscale, cleaner grocery store with more experiential offerings than your traditional grocer could provide. They had things like gourmet popcorn, an olive bar, a grill where they cooked customers' dinner, and an extensive wine selection. Up until then, we were only available on our website, Amazon, and at three or four local health food stores.

I had the good fortune of meeting Bob Mariano, the CEO of Mariano's, at a minority opportunity fair in the summer of 2014. The goal of the fair was to allow local women- and minority-owned businesses to pitch their goods and services for their new South Loop store, which was being built on the South Side of Chicago at 16th and Clark. This store was said to be a testing ground for the chain because it was located in a diverse area, not far from the side of town where the majority of African-Americans resided.

After Mr. Mariano looked over our packaging and products, he instantly said, "I want this product in our store in

West Loop in three weeks." This came as a shock to me, as well as the three buyers he was standing with, given that the fair was supposed to be solely for the South Loop store. The West Loop store, on the other hand, was in an affluent, largely white area right outside of downtown Chicago. This was a big deal. Mr. Mariano, himself, also made it clear that he wanted us in his Lake Zurich store, which is nearly fifty miles outside of Chicago in an area that was also predominantly white.

In that moment, Bob Mariano showed me that there was something bigger here than I had ever realized. This man saw far more potential in me and my company than I ever had. Up until then, I thought my products were solely meant for black women, but this experience taught me that tgin could be something bigger, a product line for everyone.

From there, our products spread throughout the Chicago-land area, not just to black neighborhoods but to diverse neighborhoods both in the city and in the suburbs. This caused me to not only rethink how I viewed the company, but how I viewed our potential growth. It also forced me to consider how I would manage to have a company that made products for everyone but was committed to the idea of celebrating the beauty of women of color, who traditional media and organizations often neglected and ignored.

After getting into Mariano's that summer, the company started to gain momentum. We had experienced a considerable amount of success, but until that big break, all of it had been online. Mariano's was our first major foray into retail, which presented an opportunity for customers to buy our products off the shelf at their local grocery store. With Mariano's came lessons about planograms, end caps, pricing, in-store promotions, and merchandising, all of which would serve me well nearly eighteen months later when we would launch in Target. This new opportunity was anything but easy. We had to drive to the store, drop off products, and put them on the shelves because we were not considered big enough to use the services of their warehouse. It was grueling but worth it because it taught me the importance of keeping your shelf merchandised and having solid relationships with store employees. It may have seemed like I was taking the long road, but I was being prepared. I was getting the training wheels I needed to handle larger opportunities and didn't even know it.

Acquiring a new business partner in Mariano's meant that I needed more help with everyday business and inventory; hires were needed, which once again meant there weren't enough funds leftover to pay me, the owner. As a result, I was a long way away from quitting my day job, and while my dad was proud to see us making gains, he didn't feel we were at a point where I could step out on my own. I was inclined to agree.

As tgin continued to gain steam, I began to realize that I was essentially an outsider in an industry that I knew very little about. I had to be careful and figure out who I could trust. Not everyone looking to give me advice or a break had my best interest at heart. There were people along the way with years of experience looking to take advantage of young companies like mine, whether asking to partner, to invest, or do a deal. In this business, one bad decision could have meant the end for me and my company. I have seen it happen, and it's not pretty.

Being a contract lawyer came in handy, but it also held me back in a lot of ways. Because of that attention to detail, I never quit my job, I was slow to hire, and I was reluctant to take major risks or sign anything, because a lot of contracts were very one-sided. Not trusting kept me safe, but it also prevented me from taking those necessary risks.

I've been in situations where people asked me to sign contracts that would have basically signed away a significant portion of my rights in the company in exchange for an introduction to a major retailer, something that I could have done weeks later without their assistance. The truth is, in this business, you could be making tons of money without taking anything home. After all of the chargebacks for unsold or returned products, deductions for promotions and in-store marketing, and middlemen who insert themselves between you and the customer, there was always some chunk of change that was owed. I was always mindful of this feeling of uncertainty, but I couldn't explain why I felt this way. I just knew that I didn't know what I didn't know, and that one bad move—one bad contract, one bad deal—could have left me bankrupt, so I was as cautious as possible, and it worked out in my favor.

In reality, the beauty business is a lot like a record business; you're going to get screwed on your first deal. How many times have we heard the stories of music artists at the height of their career, selling millions of records, and then out of nowhere, they're filing for bankruptcy? When they look back on their experiences, they realize that everyone was making money but them, and at the end of the day, they were being charged for studio time, music videos, concert tours, and legal fees, among other things. It's the same thing in any other business when you're dealing with partners. All it takes is one bad contract or investor, and everyone—and I mean, everyone—will make money but you.

The one thing I wish someone would've told me before I started on this journey, and that I tell women who are interested in breaking into the beauty game, is that it takes a million dollars to make a million dollars. A lot of people don't understand how the numbers work and are out here quitting their jobs to make hair products in their kitchen in the hopes of getting rich. It simply doesn't work that way. When you make a million dollars, 50 percent of that goes to inventory. Of that, an additional 30 percent goes to administrative costs, which leaves about 20 percent. Of this $200,000, you have to pay corporate taxes on 30 percent of this sum, leaving about $140,000. You may think that's a decent amount of money, but if your distribution is doubling, you then have to take that $140,000 and invest in inventory, marketing, and hiring more people, which means $0. Knowing your margins and studying the industry upfront can help make efficient planning and decision-making easier to ensure the longevity of your enterprise.

Back then, I was learning on the fly, so I was conservative and took it slow when it came to growing the company. Yes, I could have probably quit my job sooner, but I would have learned the hard way that even after making a million dollars, you can still go home with zero, or even in debt, which can put you in a very difficult position both personally and financially.

I had to have the ability to grow, pay other people's salaries, invest in inventory, grow our space, buy new products, and find more success, while also paying my mortgage and taking care of myself. I was scared— and rightfully so—that if I quit my job too soon we wouldn't make it, because we were growing so quickly and burning through cash as we tried to scale up our operations.

For those of you who are starting a business, this is not to say you can't quit your job to start a company and find success. Just know that the journey is long and expensive, especially at the beginning, and that you have to be careful of who you deal with along the way. If you move too quickly early on, you could lose it all. I've seen it happen.

For my situation, I didn't want to take on outside debt or investors, which meant I would have to grow a lot slower without an infusion of outside capital. I wanted to focus on keeping all of my equity in the company, thanks to the advice of a successful entrepreneur who told me that holding on to my equity was the best thing I could do for my long-term goals. Think of every percent as being worth $1 million. Because of his advice, I'm still 100 percent owner to this day.

Although I was able to dodge some bullets, I learned that I couldn't trust everyone and ended up getting burned a couple of times. When I first started selling my book, I was using a distributor who would order the book by the thousands. In the beginning, he would pay me regularly and on time, and then, after some time, the payments came to a halt. At this point, he had made thousands of dollars selling my book to various bookstores around the country, but he was unwilling to pay his outstanding invoices from me.

It was my first lesson in learning how to deal with accounts receivable and extending credit. Although I hit a bump, this experience prepared me for dealing with much larger retailer accounts. It taught me that I had to be tough when it came to collecting my coins, even if it meant refusing to ship to a customer because they had too many unpaid invoices. This situation also taught me the importance of doing credit checks, reviewing a person's standing with the Better Business Bureau, and searching the local court docket to see what cases, if any, they had pending against them.

The same could be said for the time I had to deal with one of my manufacturers. Just as my company was starting to take off, one of our contract manufacturers was facing major financial issues and was in the midst of Chapter 11 bankruptcy proceedings. While I was on a business trip to Africa, I got a phone call from one of our vendors asking if I knew about my manufacturer's financial situation. I remember telling my friend that night, "We just need to go have a drink, and I'll deal with this when I get back. There's nothing I can do about it from Tanzania."

Ultimately, everything worked out, but had I not acted quickly on my return, my little bit of an investment was going to be trapped in bankruptcy proceedings, which would have required me to obtain a court order to retrieve products I already paid for. This would have delayed shipments to some of our largest customers. I had been continually doing business with these people, and never once did they hint to me that they were facing financial troubles. In business, things change, and you should check on the health of your vendors every so often to make sure you're not putting your business in jeopardy. It's also key to have a backup plan in case someone, or something, falls through.

These are definitely the kind of problems you want to have and the lessons you want to learn when you're smaller. Had something like this happened when I had launched in Target, it could've caused tgin to be pulled from the store for having low sales because of a lack of stock. Again, thank God for the long route.

We all have goals and dreams that we hope to one day accomplish. Some days, it feels like those goals and dreams are just out of our reach. Some days, they feel like they'll never come to pass. But life has taught me that, on this journey, it's sometimes better to take the long route. Our society places tremendous value on instant everything. We constantly find ourselves crossing one finish line only to start the next. We have it in our heads that we have to hit certain milestones by a certain age, whether it's in our personal life or business, and nothing could be further from the truth. The key is to realize that life is not a race, but a journey filled with twists, turns, and pit stops along the way, many of which are preparing us for something bigger and greater. Don't rush, and trust the process.

Chapter Eight

LET GO AND LET GOD

I always say that 2015 was one of the best and worst years of my life. It's hard to think that something so amazing and something so tragic could happen in the same year. On March 1, 2015, my company launched in over 250 Target stores nationwide. This was one of our biggest milestones as a company.

I never thought, nor did these large behemoth companies ever believe, that one day they would not only be fighting for shelf space in major national retail outlets with small companies like tgin, but, in many instances, they'd be losing that fight.

The time leading up to the launch was extremely stressful.

Before the ink was dry on this deal, I literally had to gather almost every single piece of paper that was connected to my business since I gave birth to this thing. And guess what? Sometimes electronic copies or unsigned copies were not good enough. I'm talking about originals with actual signatures. I was fortunate enough to get a loan from a local community bank that believed in me. As part of that process, I was responsible for making sure all of the paperwork was in order, responding to security lien requests, and making sure any bank who loaned the company money could get their funds back if we didn't "make it." Life insurance coverage, a vial of blood, and a drug test—they wanted it all.

When placed in pretty stressful situations, I'm an amazing delegator. This time, though, I had to really roll up my sleeves and go all in because everything was so time sensitive. The sooner we delivered, the sooner we would get paid. However, if we were not on top of our game and things get delayed, it could put off when we got paid, which would make it look like we lost a ton of money at the end of the year due to all the inventory purchases. As part of the Target launch, I learned we had no control over everyone's delivery schedule. Trying to find a warehouse with fifty thousand twelve-ounce bottles lying around was seemingly impossible, but on top of that, we needed everything in less than six weeks. And yeah, those shiny silver caps that make us look luxe cost a fortune. The lead time on such a small element is super long, so we had to go out and see if we could find another supplier to help us make our deadline.

To make matters worse, our Honey Miracle Hair Mask, a deep conditioner we made by hand, was tied with our Butter Cream Daily Moisturizer for the #1 spot of best-selling product. Back then, we were doing everything by hand in small batches, working on deadlines, even when our products started to take off and hit bestseller lists.

When I came up with the idea for our Honey Miracle Hair Mask, I had no idea it would blow up and become so insanely popular. YouTube vlogger CharyJay called it her favorite deep conditioner, and people were regularly posting to Instagram about how this formula was literally the holy grail of natural hair care products. The positive reception, however, proved to be both a blessing and a curse. A blessing because it was great to have loyal customers fall in love with this amazing product. A curse because it caused difficulty in keeping up with high demands when we still made the product by hand in thirty-pound batches. Without factory-level production, we had to work hard, fast, and creatively to keep up with orders both online and in store. It was nuts.

This scramble to produce product was exaggerated by the size of our team; we gave new meaning to the term "lean startup." Our entire production department was run by just two people. They were responsible for cranking out thousands of shea butters, argan oils, soaps, and our best-selling Honey Miracle Hair Mask on a monthly basis. So when we received our first Target order and my team said, "Boss Lady, we got this," I wondered whether they expected me to believe they weren't on something.

Given the size of the order and the tight deadlines we were working under, we brought in a team of temps to support my production team, helping with bottling, labeling, and boxing up our products. Even I rolled up my sleeves and got in there. Overnight, I went from CEO to production manager, which meant I was cracking that whip in an effort to get 2,000 units cranked out, boxed, and labeled each day. Let me tell you, pushing out 2,000 units a day is a major feat when you're using a handheld Oster mixer. Those little mixers are intended for that little batch of brownies that you make four times a year, not for running on high six to eight hours a day. Working on our first Target order showed me just how hard production is. When I say production is hard, I mean it's **HARD**. Being on your feet all day long, mixing products by hand for hours on end, and putting labels on 10,000 jars is more than most could handle. I have always had major respect for my production team, but the time and effort that went into making thousands of jars of product by hand is enough to make you want to hang up your apron and tell Boss Lady where she can shove her mixer.

As production manager and CEO, I inspected every single product for quality. This was our first big order, and I couldn't afford to make mistakes. If this order wasn't right or if it was delivered late, we could suffer a major financial setback. As a result, I made it a point to touch every product that was made and seal every single box that went onto the final pallet. If the product felt too light, I made the team add more. If a label was on crooked, it had to be reapplied. If a label contained an air bubble, it had to be readjusted. If the ink on the label was off, scrap it. I wasn't playing. My name and our reputation were on the line.

I put a lot of stress on myself, and to make matters worse, I didn't have a healthy way of channeling it. I was literally working nonstop.

Target was our biggest break yet. I had been grinding for years, and it seemed like my work was finally starting to pay off. I had made so many sacrifices, and we finally made it. Our sales climbed, and we started to reach our customers from a more grassroots standpoint instead of solely having an online presence.

Being in Target gave the company a legitimacy that we hadn't had before when we were just selling online and at local farmers' markets. We were one of the few small, up-and-coming beauty brands, but Target helped to put us on the map. When we were able to close that deal, people started to look at us differently. We were a real company, a real business. At that moment, it felt like things were finally settling into place.

After getting into Target, I felt that the company had finally reached a place where I could pull back some and start to focus on my personal life and actually give some consideration to starting a serious relationship. I even thought I was at the point where I could give serious thought to settling down and starting a family.

For so long, I had put off having kids or marriage. I always felt that being in a serious relationship required effort and compromise, and I wasn't willing to put my dreams on hold for anyone or take a back seat for anyone else's goals. I had a clear end game in mind, and I was focused. I was thirty-six, and while most women would have been frantic about getting married by the time they'd turned thirty, that wasn't the case for me. I had extreme tunnel vision and was intensely focused on building my company. I wanted to get tgin to the point where I felt comfortable with my success and was able to make compromises if I had a partner or children. Call me selfish, but I'm just being honest.

When I turned thirty-five, I made the decision to freeze my eggs. I decided to attend a presentation on fertility preservation sponsored by the Junior League of Chicago. After hearing the doctor speak about his success with IVF and IUI with women who chose to harvest their eggs, I decided it was better to be safe than sorry. But when I discussed the whole idea with my OBGYN, she acted as if I was crazy. She said I was young and healthy and that she had many patients who had given birth in their early forties. She told me that the only circumstance where she would advise a young patient to do so was if she had cancer. Against her advice, I went ahead and had the procedure done. Thank God I did.

I was feeling the pressure of wanting a family at some point, but I was not totally ready. I wanted more in my personal life, but I wasn't ready to jump from juggling my day job and running a company to changing diapers and cleaning Cheerios off the back seat of my car overnight. Landing the Target deal led me to believe I was getting closer and closer to being able to have more work-life balance, but nothing could have been further from the truth.

Chapter Nine

THE BIG TEST

I found a lump.

People often ask me how I found out I had cancer. It was simple. In the summer of 2015, I discovered a lump one day while showering; it was in my right breast. Initially, I thought it was hormone-related. Some days, it seemed smaller or as if it wasn't there, while other days, it seemed to be getting bigger. It was soft and movable and not at all concerning initially. After several months, however, it became clear that it wasn't going away.

Although I wasn't completely ignoring it, I never gave serious consideration to the idea that it could be cancer.

I remember going to one of my best friends' birthday party in Palm Springs that October. After going for a swim and taking a shower, I could feel that the lump was getting noticeably bigger. I mentioned it to her, and she told me to go see my gynecologist. When I got back home, I made an appointment, but they told me I couldn't get in for three weeks. I told my friend, and she said, "No, you need to actually tell them what's going on and see if you can get in right away." So I did exactly that, and they saw me immediately.

When I went in, I wasn't afraid of anything. Business was good, I was starting to have a personal life again, and I felt like I was floating on cloud nine. I had no inkling of what I was up against. Breast cancer never crossed my mind as a real possibility. I was young, black, healthy, and in pretty good shape. To top it off, I had no family history of breast cancer. What did I have to be afraid of?

During the appointment, my gynecologist examined me and felt the lump. Because of its size, softness, and mobility, and the lack of pain, discharge, or dimpling, she didn't suspect cancer. Still, she ordered a mammogram for a few weeks later, just to be on the safe side.

I left that day and returned to my normal, everyday life. Three weeks later, I went in for the mammogram wearing my Superwoman crop top, thinking it'd be a great Instagram moment—"Ladies, check your boobs." I thought nothing of it. During the exam, the X-ray tech started the mammogram, and things were going according to plan. But then, her voice got shaky, and she called in the radiologist to review the images. At that moment, I knew something wasn't right.

After taking multiple images, the tech escorted me into another room and had me meet with the doctor. The doctor reviewed my films and said she would like for me to come back the next day. When I asked them why, they said they saw something "suspicious," something "concerning," which I later learned are carefully chosen words that the medical profession uses when they suspect there is a malignancy. When I asked them to clarify what they meant by "suspicious" and "concerning," the doctor told me that she saw an architectural distortion on my X-ray and that she wanted to do a biopsy the next day.

That night, I went home and googled "architectural distortion." I stayed up late, trying to better understand my condition for when I returned the following day. I read all kinds of message boards and scientific studies on the presence of architectural distortions on mammograms. From what I was reading, I could tell it didn't look good, but I had faith. I struggled with whether to share the news with my dad, but I decided to hold off to prevent him from worrying in case nothing was wrong.

The next day, I came back with a friend, armed with my research.

Unlike the day before, for this appointment, I had to wait. While sitting in the waiting room, I came to the realization that I was at a hospital where I probably shouldn't have gone. The best healthcare in Chicago can be found on the Gold Coast, where rich, white people live, and I was on the South Side of Chicago at a community hospital. As I sat in the waiting room, I overheard many of the conversations and quickly learned that many of the women being seen at this hospital were on government insurance and some were without insurance altogether. The one thing we all had in common was that we were scared.

When it was my turn to see the doctor, I wasn't feeling very optimistic, and the depressing waiting room, with its outdated furniture, old magazines, and frightened uninsured women, only made things worse.

After performing a biopsy, I had a very frank conversation with the doctor and asked a series of in-depth questions based on my research. After my long night spent with Dr. Google, I knew that weird shape was most likely cancer, so I asked about it. I asked about the size of the mass and where it fell on the BIRAD scale—one is good, four is concerning, and five is probably cancer.[1] She gave me a 4C. *Fuck. I might have cancer.* I could tell by her reaction that she wasn't used to patients asking a lot of questions or asking super involved ones. It was a brief conversation, and I didn't leave there with a lot of hope. She told me she would call me in two days with the results.

When I left the hospital with my friend, she told me everything would be okay and that there was no way I had cancer; I was too young. I wanted to believe her, but deep down, I knew something was amiss.

Once I made it back to my car, I called my dad from the parking lot and told him the deal. I had made the decision not to share the information with him earlier because I didn't want him to worry if the lump turned out to be a false alarm. I tried to lean on my girlfriends, but I really needed my dad to be there for me. I just didn't want to scare him. These conversations can be difficult to have, particularly with men, when you're talking about something like breast cancer.

But here I was, thirty-six, alone, and waiting for someone to call me and tell me whether I had cancer or not. I pulled it together like I always did and told him what

---

1   BI-RADS stands for Breast Imaging Reporting and Data System and was established by the American College of Radiology. BI-RADS is a scheme for putting the findings from mammogram screening (for breast cancer diagnosis) into a small number of well-defined categories.

the situation was looking like. I wanted to tell him it was nothing, but I blurted out, "It doesn't look good." I didn't have the strength in me to hold up the appearance that everything was okay when it wasn't. I was scared, and all I could think about was what was going to happen to me.

After going over everything the doctor said with my father, we agreed that my situation would just be between the two of us. Although he took the news well when I told him, I knew that he was back on the phone minutes after we hung up, calling his sisters in North Carolina and telling them there could be something wrong with me. Given my mom's personal battle with cancer and that this had to do with my female parts, he had nowhere to turn for real guidance about what this all meant.

Pretty soon, I was getting random texts from my aunts asking about the weather in Chicago and how I was doing. I knew he'd told them, but I wasn't mad. I understood that he needed someone he could talk to during this difficult time.

Immediately after calling my dad, I rang my uncle, Willie. Originally from Texas, he moved to Detroit at the age of twenty to become an electrician in one of the auto plants. That's when he and my dad became friends. Although Willie is not my blood relative, he's been my dad's close friend for fifty-plus years and has become like my substitute mom. During my childhood, he lived with my family off and on and eventually landed in his own place.

When he answered the phone, I broke down crying.

"Willie, I went to the doctor. They think I might have breast cancer," I sobbed. In his usual slow-talking fashion, he reassured me with his thick Texan accent that I shouldn't get myself worked up and that we were all going to get through this together.

After I made it home, I waited for the phone to ring with the results. I'm not the type of person who can keep herself busy or do laundry to keep my mind off a cancer diagnosis, so I literally just laid there. In hindsight, I wish I would've asked my doctor for medication to help with the anxiety. It was torture unlike anything I had ever experienced before. I would later learn that at Northwestern Hospital, patients are generally told of their results the same day to help cut down on the stress of waiting, and here I was waiting forty-eight hours. But I was at a community safety-net hospital on the South Side of Chicago, and that's the kind of service you get when you're underinsured.

Those forty-eight hours were the longest and hardest of my life. I literally sat in the dark for almost two days with candles burning, surrounded by affirmations, like

"The devil is a liar," and "Don't doubt, just believe." I was hoping that keeping my mind positive would somehow have a spiritual impact on the universe.

In these types of situations, my lawyer knowledge kicks in, and I know that it's better to be proactive to get what I really want. Waiting was killing me, and I was basically losing my mind. So, after thirty-six hours, I called the nurse back. She told me that my results had come back in and that she would have the doctor call me. When she said that, I knew it was probably bad news.

About fifteen minutes later, my doctor called me to say, "Chris-Tia, I'm sorry, but you have invasive ductile carcinoma."

After that, I just stopped listening.

Three hours after the call, I was picking my dad up from the airport. I was so scared about what all of this meant that I slept in the bed with my dad those first two nights after receiving the news. I hadn't done that since I was three or four years old, but now, I was a thirty-six-year-old woman sleeping in the bed with her dad. I was weak.

He brought his Bible with him on this trip and into every appointment I had after that. He flew to Chicago twelve times to go with me to each of my appointments, whether he was living in Michigan or Florida. He was there by my side to support me through this tremendous, life-threatening health challenge.

While my mom made the decision to continue working while she had cancer, my dad and I decided that I would take a nine-month leave of absence from Oracle, so I could focus on my health. Although my dad has always held my mom on a pedestal and felt she could do no wrong, I needed permission to alleviate the pressure of juggling working full time as a corporate lawyer and running tgin with my diagnosis. My dad helped me see that I didn't need to live up to my mom's perceived strength and that we needed to break the cycle and allow my body to heal and rest. This one decision would ultimately give me the peace, time, and space I needed to take off my cape and rethink a lot of things I did just like my mom had, including how I process my emotional issues and deal with vulnerability. Still, my thoughts were constantly on my mom and family, on what would happen with my company, and what would happen to me.

When I was first diagnosed with breast cancer, I initially thought, *Why me? Why now?* Given my mom's experience with a different kind of cancer, I thought if I did have to go down that path, it'd be when I was fifty or older. My mom's life and my own had so many parallels, from how we look to how we act and communicate. I never thought cancer would come for me so soon. To make matters worse, cancer doesn't run in our family, but we were both fortunate enough to be "blessed" with this so-called gift. How could we be the only two people in our family willed to go through this same situation? It's important to be hopeful, but it's difficult in that scenario.

People often think of their parents and role models when placed in tough situations, and I was no exception. Especially for people who lose a parent early, we're always measuring our own mortality against our parent's. If they die of a heart attack at forty-five, many people feel like they can't live life on their terms until they've passed that age. Not only did I have to fight cancer, but I had to fight this mental battle of thinking I would be dead in a year. That's how the journey was for my mom.

Once I got cancer, there was always that whisper in the back of my mind. Even though we had two different types of cancer, I just didn't know what my actual prognosis would be. My mom was here today and gone a year later. That was a hard pill to swallow. It could be me this time. Even though I'm still here two, going on three years later, it's still hard. My dad won't say it, but I think he is still on pins and needles. Nonetheless, the survival rate for most cases of breast cancer diagnosed early is well over 95 percent, so I have a lot to be grateful for.

* * *

The day I received my diagnosis was the same day that tgin was supposed to have its annual company holiday dinner at Wildfire, one of Chicago's favorite steakhouses. I enjoy being out with my team, celebrating over a vodka tonic. That year, we had an amazing year in Target and would be launching in 500 Sally Beauty Supply stores just two weeks later.

But I couldn't pull it together.

I debated for hours whether to have the party and give my team the celebration they deserved, before I decided to pull the plug. As much as I wanted to, I couldn't muster up the strength to put on a happy face when I was dealing with such tragic news. There would be no merry-making or celebrations when I had what could be a fatal disease at thirty-six years old. I was scared out of my mind.

When I looked at the faces of breast cancer in the media, they were always images of older, white women, not black ones. When I thought of cancer, I thought of names like Shannen Doherty, Melissa Etheridge, Sheryl Crow, or Christina Applegate. The people featured on *Good Morning America* or the Avon Walk never looked like me. The Beyoncés, Gabrielle Unions, and Tracee Ellis Rosses of the world don't get cancer. Other than *Good Morn-*

ing America anchor, Robin Roberts, I never saw a lot of black women openly dealing with this condition. We were totally missing from the conversation, which was not only odd, but it made me feel even more alone.

They say you're either in a storm, coming out of a storm, or about to go into a storm. I felt like I was in some version of all three.

After receiving my diagnosis, I had to make a follow-up visit with a breast surgeon at the safety net hospital on the South Side to go over my options and decide whether I would have a lumpectomy or a mastectomy. During our consultation, one of the first things she told me was, "Given your breast cancer type and your age, you'll have to take a pill for ten years. You're not going to be able to have kids during this time." Telling me that I was not going to be able to have kids until forty-six was like saying I wasn't going to be able to have kids at all.

I broke down completely. I laid on the table in the doctor's room in the fetal position, while my dad sat there beside me clutching his Bible. The timing seemed like a cruel joke. Things were turning around professionally; I finally felt like I could quit my job at Oracle, and my skills were at a high level. I was thinking about starting a family. I worked so hard building this company to leave a legacy for myself and my kids, and now, I was facing the possibility that everything I worked for was for nothing. I had no one to leave this entity that I poured my heart and soul into to. That was one of the hardest things for me to come to grips with. I had even met a guy whom I was really into and seemed emotionally available for. Our relationship was just starting to blossom. And now this.

* * *

My family was always spiritual. Growing up, I went to church every Sunday. I even made an effort to go regularly when I was in college, then well into my professional career. One of my favorite Bible verses is Proverbs 3:5, which says, "Trust in the Lord with all your heart and lean not on your own understanding." I read my Bible every morning, and thought I knew what it meant to trust God, but when I was hit with this devastating news, my world was turned upside down, and I didn't have the strength to open my Bible, pray, or turn to God. I stopped going to church shortly thereafter.

I didn't see any light at the end of the tunnel, and if I could have just died, I would have. I decided to call my sister, whom I had barely spoken to in years, and asked her to pray for me. Now, here I was with my life hanging in the balance. Despite our issues, my sister was a prayer warrior. She has a way of getting in the spirit like no one else in our family, and I came to her asking her to cover me in prayer.

Sometimes, when you're most in need of prayer, you're not the best one to do it. Your head is too crowded with fear and anger and a sense of injustice and guilt. Sometimes asking others to pray for you when you feel like you can't is a lifesaver. God knows that you're scared, and he knows what you need and will answer others' prayers for you.

My dad was also one of those people who was consistently there to lift my spirits. He was always reading his Bible, whether he was in my presence or not. Deep down inside, I knew I wasn't alone. Even though he was strong for me on this journey, I could tell how hard it was on him to have to deal with this a second time. First with my mom, and now with me.

* * *

December 22 was the day I met with the breast surgeon who led me to believe I was incapable of having kids. The next day, my dad found something in his *Daily Word* devotional that completely changed my outlook. On Wednesday, December 23, he handed me a small sheet of paper that talked about the story of when the angel Gabriel visited Mary and told her that she would soon bear a child. The message in those words spoke about amazing things happening in my own life, leaving me in a similar state of mixed emotions. It ended with, "I open my heart to receive miracles." After handing me that scripture, my dad told me we'd get through this together if we stayed focused and faithful. He said he'd be there for me the entire way and that it'd be a journey. At that point, I realized that this battle was not mine but the Lord's, and that if motherhood was in the cards for me, it was going to be a miracle.

Growing up, my parents provided me with a powerful example of black love, which is why I have been so unwilling to settle when it comes relationships and getting married.

When my mom graduated from college and passed the CPA exam, she was forced to open her own accounting firm. No accounting firm would take a chance and hire her because she was young, black, and inexperienced.

To Marie Farrell-Donaldson
With best wishes,

Ronald Reagan

My mom was invited to the White House by Presidents Ronald Reagan and
George Bush. Growing up, seeing my mom shake hands with presidents of the
United States created a lot of pressure on me to be successful.

Growing up in a predominantly black city and seeing black lawyers, doctors, and millionaires gave me a lot of confidence, which is not always a good thing for black women in certain spaces.

My mom died just thirty days after I graduated from high school and two months before I started my freshman year at Harvard.

After graduating from Harvard Law School, I moved to Chicago to practice corporate law at one of the nation's most prestigious law firms—the one where Barack and Michelle Obama met.

I had an opportunity to meet and have lunch with the legendary Johnnie Cochran, the lead defense lawyer in the O.J. Simpson trial, during my time at Harvard. Famous people were always on campus engaging with students and networking with professors about cutting edge topics in the legal, business, and technological realms.

I opted to wear a wig when I started my first job to hide my kinky-curl hair, believing that it would give me more opportunities and a greater chance of becoming partner.

For years, I would spend every Saturday on my feet in a tgin t-shirt and black shorts selling books, t-shirts, and shea butters at local summer festivals around the Chicago area.

After many years of being scared, I finally made the decision to step out on faith and release my own products.

When I was diagnosed with breast cancer, cutting my hair was hard, but I had to focus on putting my health first. After completing treatment, I was insecure about the fact that I had to wear a wig when I was the head of a natural hair company.

Seeing my products on Target shelves for the first time was the most incredible feeling.

On March 1, 2016, I had my first chemo treatment. Two weeks later, I would travel to Minneapolis to give my first presentation to the buyer at Target.

On March 15, 2016, after receiving my first chemo treatment, I traveled to Minneapolis to meet with the Target buyer and discuss our year one financial performance. While I was undergoing treatment, our revenues doubled, and door count quadrupled. God is good!

One week after finishing cancer treatments, I booked a ticket to Bali to find out why my life was so hectic and why I never put myself first.

Today, the tgin Foundation uses its success in the beauty space to raise awareness of breast cancer health disparities due to race and socio-economic factors, and to empower young women to listen to their bodies. We have raised over $50,000 to date towards free mammograms, breast navigation outreach services, and raising awareness of the importance of early detection using our tgin Pink Ambassador Program.

Chapter Ten

INVISIBLE HAND

Before my treatment plan was identified, I spent a lot of time on websites and in chat rooms where women were talking about the side effects of their treatments. They talked about gaining thirty pounds, losing movement in their legs and fingers, having dry vaginas and no sex drive, growing back thinner hair when all was said and done. After reading so much negativity, I was a wreck thinking about it all. Even if I made it out, what type of woman would I be, especially as a woman trying to run a hair care company? I wasn't sure if living sounded that awesome. In fact, at that point, dying didn't sound half bad.

I was trying to search for answers as to what my situation meant and what my outcome would be. I soon realized that all of that just fed into the negativity. Everything comes down to perspective and how you choose to see the world. Is the glass half full or half empty? I had to force myself to remember the scripture my dad gave, which said I had to be open to receiving miracles.

Although I had some bad days, especially early on, I made a conscious decision to see what was happening to me from a positive perspective, in a more "half full" light. I tuned out all the negative experiences people had and just focused on fighting my own battles. How was I ever going to make it through this journey if I was constantly allowing people's negative energy to feed my spirit along the way?

When you're a businesswoman, sometimes you can get so focused on what your competitors are doing that you can't see your own strategy. The same is true in the personal realm. We're often so caught up in the filtered version of other people's lives, vacations, relationships, marriages, or babies that we can't even live or enjoy our own lives. I had to completely transform my thinking and focus on my own health if I was going to win this battle.

Based on the characteristics of each person's cancer, the doctors develop a cocktail that is customized to attack a person's specific tumor and prevent it from replicating itself or spreading. It comes down to the biology of a patient's tumor, age, health history, weight, how fast it's growing, and where it's located. There are so many variables. My cancer was ER+, PR+, HER2–, Grade 3, Stage 2b. I quickly realized that I couldn't compare my cancer to anybody else's cancer. I had Chris-Tia's cancer, and the doctors had to deal with that specifically, which meant I had to tune out all the negativity and the different challenges people were facing on the message boards.

That realization gave me the strength to stop focusing on the outcome and start focusing more on the day-to-day, since so much of it was outside of my control. Before I even began to think about beating it, I had to have a positive attitude. I had to decide to let go and let God. Even today, with whatever difficulties I'm facing, this is something I have to remember. I'm not in control of everything, or even most things for that matter.

When I was first scheduled to begin treatment after completing my surgery, I had a meeting with my oncologist. She said, "When can you start chemotherapy?" Even though I had Stage 2 cancer (which meant it had not spread to my lymph nodes), they wanted to be aggressive because of my age and the growth pattern of my cancer. My doctor concluded that full chemotherapy and radiation would be best for me. When a patient is older, the doctors don't have to be as aggressive because cancers in older individuals tend to grow more slowly.

When I came to grips with the fact that I had to have

chemotherapy, I was scared as hell. I read a lot of crazy things about the Red Devil, which is cancer slang for Adriamycin. It causes nausea, vomiting, weight loss, and constipation, and I had to prepare myself mentally and physically for this literal battle with the devil.

After meeting with my oncology team for the first time, they gave me a giant three-ring binder that described all the negative side effects of chemotherapy, both during treatment and long-term. The side effects (both short-term and long-term) ranged from vaginal dryness, loss of libido, and weight gain to hair loss, nausea, loss of feeling in my legs and fingers, hot flashes, etc. Alongside the information I'd read in message boards, I was certain I would go from a perfectly normal, healthy, in-shape thirty-six-year-old woman running her own company to looking and feeling like a post-menopausal sixty-year-old lady, most likely staying that way for the rest of my life. That night, I felt like I would never again be the woman I once was and that, without kids to call my own, I didn't really have much to fight for.

It was Super Bowl Sunday the day I received this news. I'm not one to cry or have breakdowns, but I was at my weakest moment ever. I felt sorry for myself and was thinking once again, *Why me? How unfair.* Although I was seeing a therapist on and off during this time to help deal with my diagnosis, I had tons of pent-up frustration, both at the world and at God. I wanted to end it all. I felt I had nothing other than my dad to live for. I didn't want to fight, and I didn't have a lot of hope. I had reached my breaking point, literally and figuratively.

I've never had much of a temper, but that night, I was angry. I wanted to throw my iPhone across the room, but then my inner logic took hold. I thought long and hard about denting my newly painted walls and the ordeal of living with a cracked screen for the next few days until I had time to make an appointment to go to the Apple store. So instead, I had the bright idea to kick in my glass shower door straight Bruce Lee style. Brilliant! Upon impact, the door shattered into a million little pieces. Shards of glass flew everywhere. It was exactly what I needed. A release. I had a long, hard, ugly cry.

I share this only because, so many times, I would look at other patients on Instagram at the beginning of my journey, and everyone looked so happy going to chemotherapy. They called themselves "fighters," and all I could think was, *This is some bullshit*. I was fucking pissed that God had chosen me to go through this. After what my mom went through, it never crossed my mind that he might have a plan to give me beauty for ashes.

Sometimes life breaks you, and you have to find a way to pick up the pieces and put yourself back together again.

Sometimes, you are at your lowest point, and the thought of being your old "happy" self again seems completely impossible. Maybe you're asking, "Why me God?" I know I did. Most of us would rather live without enduring a season of pain. Yet during such difficult times, God often does His greatest work in our lives.

When I look back on that moment of me laying on the floor of my bathroom, sobbing, and compare it to who I am today, it is a powerful reminder of how far I have come. That day, I really didn't think I was going to make it. I didn't see God's plan for my life. But here I am, years later after enduring so much. I'm stronger than ever, back at work, falling in love with myself, and using my darkest hour to help others find courage and be inspired to take care of themselves physically, spiritually, and emotionally.

Before that moment, I hadn't really cried. I'd been super-woman, but I couldn't do that anymore. In that moment, I gave myself permission to be angry, to be sad, to be everything I'd never given myself permission to be. I've always been so buttoned up. Be sad but keep working. Be happy but keep working. Be depressed but keep working. In that moment, I unleashed it all. It was just what I needed to keep going and start fighting for my life. I had to decide whether I was going to be a cancer patient and focus on the negative, or trust that everything would work out for the best. I decided to move forward with my life and accept what this test was meant to teach me.

* * *

When I met with my oncologist after my lumpectomy weeks later, we decided on my chemo schedule, making sure to note any important dates I couldn't miss. We decided on March 1, 2016, for my first session because I had a super important meeting with Target on March 22, my first in-person meeting with the buyer since the launch. The doctor said that it would be early enough in my treatment that I would be able to recover from my second chemo session on March 15 and still look good when I met with the Target team. At that point, I thought I had cancer under control and that my doctor and I had it figured out. After the Target meeting, I thought I'd be on cruise control and totally chill out and do nothing but the bare minimum for tgin.

When the Target meeting came around, though, I was scared to death. Even though giving presentations is one of my greatest strengths and I'm normally very confident, I was incredibly nervous that day. In the first fifteen seconds of our appointment, I could feel my voice shaking a little bit. To top it off, no one in the room knew I was dealing with breast cancer. Thankfully, almost two minutes into my presentation, my confidence came back out of nowhere. When I was done, as one of the last brands they saw for the day, the key compliment they gave me was, "Now that's how you give a presentation." I had nailed it.

The Target team was impressed, and I felt like I was back to my old self for the first time since receiving my diagnosis in December. Maybe I wasn't all the way back, but I started to realize I was more than just a cancer patient. That meeting helped me realize that I couldn't allow cancer to be the one thing that defined me. I was still a daughter, a sister, a businesswoman, a CEO. I was still an attorney, a boss, and a friend. I still enjoyed cooking, shopping, keeping my house clean, and binge-watching episodes of Sex and the City. Cancer wasn't all of me; it was just a piece of me.

Three weeks after meeting with Target, I had two more chemotherapy treatments. I looked a mess. I had lost a ton of weight, the color was gone from my skin, and it looked like I hadn't slept in days, but it didn't matter, because I didn't have to interact with anyone for business other than brief communication with my team over email and the phone. Then, even more breakthroughs started coming in. We got an email that said we were in Whole Foods. After years of doing paperwork trying to get into Whole Foods and sending them at least twenty emails, none of which got returned, of course we finally hear from them when I'm dealing with a major setback.

Three weeks after that, we got into Rite Aid. Then, six weeks after that, I got the opportunity to present to Walgreens. That email came in on a Tuesday while I was at the hospital receiving chemotherapy, and they wanted me to come in two days later on Thursday. With chemo, side effects kick in like clockwork forty-eight hours after the treatment. Here I had thought I could make it through the Target meeting and then chill. Turns out, that was not the case. So, I pulled it together and put my navy blue dress and wig back on. Luckily, Walgreens headquarters is in the suburbs of Chicago, so I could drive to the appointment instead of fly. When it came time for the meeting, I went in there and gave a similar presentation and was out. This time, however, I literally almost passed out on my way home from exhaustion.

When we make plans, God laughs, right? I had worked and sacrificed for years, only to get into Target, Rite Aid, Whole Foods, Walgreens, and more Sally Beauty Supply stores while I was lying on my couch. I was in disbelief. I had one plan, and God had a different one. I think He used this time to humble me and show me that despite all I had done to make my own success happen, He was still in control. My advances and my company's growth were all in His hands.

By the time I finished chemotherapy, we were doing more business than when I had been working two full-time jobs and making product for orders larger than we were equipped to handle. That was a clear message to me that sometimes you have to let go. God was truly in control. His invisible hand was running the company.

By the end of the year, our sales had doubled, and the number of doors we were in nationwide had quadrupled. My team ran the day-to-day business. All those years of me being picky, focusing on how we put labels on bottles, how we ship packages, how we respond to emails, and all of that perfectionism finally came in handy. They were able to run the business as if I were still there, almost seamlessly. I wasn't able to focus on marketing as much, but my team kept us going while I was in treatment. I would go to radiation every single day for thirty-three days in a row, and opportunities were coming in left and right.

This experience taught me that true faith means letting go completely and relying on Him to be in total control. The company that I spent nearly ten years working on could have collapsed while I was fighting cancer, or all of those side effects that I read about could have come to pass, but none of these situations even came close to happening. All along, God was telling me, "I was going to take care of this anyway. All you had to do was just believe."

In this life, our faith will be tested. I had thought for so long that, because I went to church almost every Sunday and gave my tithes and offerings, I was a good Christian woman, a believer. And while all of that shows my commitment to God and helps with the maintenance of our relationship, cancer ultimately tested my faith like no other experience had, other than my mother's death.

Up until this time, I naïvely believed that I was a woman of God who was truly grounded in her faith. Although I gave credit to God for my academic and professional accomplishments, I still believed that my hard work and discipline were also significant contributing factors to my success. Cancer, however, forced me to let go completely and showed me that when I wasn't capable of doing anything—and I mean anything—not only did God cover me, but He also filled my storehouse when it could have run empty. During this season of rest, He revealed to me that even without me, He was able and didn't need me, but, more than anything, I needed Him.

Chapter Eleven

FAMILY MATTERS

Growing up, my grandma Lolo would always say, "There's nothing more important than family." My grandmother and I have always been at odds in terms of our definition of family, and I've always questioned her willingness to accept deplorable behavior from people just because they're family. She'd say, "I don't care if they did you wrong. They're still your family." She was old school and came from a generation where you loved hard and unconditionally.

I tend to be more logical than emotional, so I've always struggled with forgiveness and the idea that family can do no wrong. Blood or not, I felt that people should do right by one another, and under no circumstances do you allow anyone to take advantage of you. If someone had done me wrong, I didn't care if they were family, I was cutting them off. This was a little extreme and very immature, but I think part of this was due to my unwillingness to show vulnerability. The other part was my way of proving that I was a superwoman and incapable of being walked over.

Over the years, I had left a trail of unresolved relationships with family and friends as a result of cutting people off left and right. When I received my diagnosis, I wasn't talking to my sister, my cousin who was like my sister, and my niece. We had all fallen out with each other over petty little things. Although I missed them, I was prideful and didn't feel like I should reach out. I felt aggrieved. This was true with most people I dealt with. Something went wrong, and I wouldn't take time to make it right. tgin came first; everything and everyone else came second. I often chose to avoid conflict and not deal with those kind of issues, and as a result, I was never truly able to let go of past hurts.

When my life was hanging in the balance, I realized that I didn't know how things were going to turn out, and I needed my family to be there for me. I had to shift my thinking and realize that family had to start being a priority.

I come from a family of strong women, where crying and showing emotion is not all that common. Even with that kind of standard, I was still viewed as one of the strongest women in my family. I was a leader, successful, and didn't take a lot of shit from people. During my diagnosis, even though I wanted family to be there for me, especially the people I was on the outs with, I was too scared to let anyone other than my dad and my Uncle Willie see me be that weak.

On one hand, I longed to feel the warmth, closeness, and intimacy of having my family close and supporting me. On the other hand, I struggled with taking off my cape, if you will, and letting people see me at my lowest and most vulnerable state. I wasn't the Superwoman they thought I was, and this was going to be a tough battle and long road for me.

I would allow my family to talk to me on the phone and send me text messages, but I wouldn't let them interact with me in person. I didn't want them to see me with my head scarf on, looking skinny, tired, or weak. Even though my family assured me that the hard feelings were behind us and we just needed to focus on my health, I didn't feel like I was able to. I was still too prideful to allow them to truly and fully be there for me. They were willing to be the bigger people, and I wasn't there yet. I didn't want to feel like I owed anyone or that I was the one being petty, and now, look at where I was.

When I thought back to when my mom had cancer, I saw

only strength. She had dinner on the table every night and still managed to raise a teenage girl with raging hormones and a horrible attitude. I never saw her cry, complain, or even look unhappy as it pertained to her health. It was like everything was normal in her world. Given her lack of openness and vulnerability, I struggled to project the same strength.

FORGIVENESS AS A TEST

When I speak on panels, people always ask how I beat cancer. They ask whether I changed my diet, whether I eat all organic foods now, and whether I cut back on drinking. The funny thing is that I was already super healthy before I got cancer. I worked out five days a week religiously, had eaten no red meat or chicken for seven years, and yet, here I was with cancer. I'm not going to lie, I drank way too much, but now, I've made a point to cut back. I was hyper-focused on the physically healthy, natural lifestyle, but not so much on being a good person or dealing with conflict.

When illness strikes, we're often quick to examine our diets or exercise regimens but fail to examine how our past hurt, trauma, or emotional conflict impacts our health. Sometimes, it's not the diet that gives you cancer, it's being a petty-ass bitch that does. Likewise, feeling the pressure to be everything to everyone and walk around like a Superwoman can also take its toll.

As a strong black woman, I often felt like I couldn't let my guard down; I couldn't let people walk over me. As a result, my relationships with my family and friends suffered greatly. I didn't want to look like a sucker. It was more important for me to be right. I was strong enough to cut people off but not strong enough to tell people that they had hurt me.

I strongly believe that holding onto grudges and not forgiving can affect our bodies on a cellular level and may contribute to diseases. People are often taken aback by this. You can go to SoulCycle every day and spend all this time working out. You can give up red meat and be completely vegan, but if you're still unwilling to let go of past hurt and wrongs, it's just as bad on your mental health. We must talk about forgiveness and the harm of holding grudges. We must talk about how important it is to lighten our load and send people away in peace. Forgiveness was yet another test for me.

Along this journey, I had to learn how to forgive not only those who had wronged me, but also myself. I had to accept the reality that I wasn't perfect and that I make mistakes just like everyone else. I couldn't continue to cut people off over the smallest slights, especially my family members. I had to look at the relationships that were important to me and give them the same love, attention, care, and focus as I did my company.

A FRIEND BEYOND FAMILY

My Uncle Willie is a seventy-seven-year-old man who smokes a pack of Marlboro Lights a day and drinks anything that isn't nailed down. He has helped me with the business in some form or fashion since day one, whether it was putting my tent up at the local farmers' market, keeping an eye on the factory when I had to work at Oracle, or travel for business. He'd take the trash out, fix our label machine, you name it.

During treatments, Uncle Willie and my dad traded off chemotherapy sessions. My dad would fly in for some sessions, and Willie would travel back and forth to Detroit to take me to others until he made the decision to move to Chicago permanently. Having Willie around was like having another parent who allowed me to totally be myself.

When my dad came to visit, I never let him see me bald. He always saw me with my head covered with a wig or hat or scarf. I wanted and needed him there, but I knew it would be too much for him to also have to deal with the sick version of his daughter. Willie, on the other hand, could handle seeing me at my worst and was there the day I kicked my shower door in.

Although it probably hurt him to see me like that, he was strong enough to handle it and was always there for me.

He was super sweet and nurturing, often coming by with food or anything else I needed. He'd spend the night in my apartment and sleep outside of my bedroom when I was scared to be alone. When he was keeping a close eye on the factory, he made sure people came to work, opened the door for my employees, and ensured that pallets got out the door on time. I felt so much love from him and appreciated everything he did. Though he wasn't my actual family, having him there made all the difference and gave me the peace of mind to sit back, relax, and do nothing but focus on my health and the faith to believe him when he said, *"Everything's gonna be alright, Chris-Tia."*

GIRLFRIENDS ARE FOREVER

While many of the friendships I made since moving to Chicago have run their course, my Harvard girlfriends have always been my lifelong friends. Our relationships were maintained mostly over text or seeing each other once a year at a reunion or some type of event. Once I found out I had cancer, these relationships became even more important to me. Because I had so much time on my hands when I was not in doctor's appointments, I was able to connect and engage with them in a way that I otherwise was unable to when I was healthy and working.

My fondest memories of being sick were spending time

on the phone, laughing and catching up with my girl-friends. Cancer became a blessing because it gave me an opportunity to appreciate the people I've met and built sisterly bonds with over the years, especially the people I went to college with. These are the people that I know will always be there for me. In our lives, those three-hour conversations are not only precious, but they root us back to who we really are at our core. I wish my current days still allowed for those conversations, but at least now, I'm getting better at reaching out and deciding that work can wait sometimes.

Cancer taught me that our sister friends can be good for the soul. They fed me. All too often, people become busy with running a company, traveling all over the place, dating someone new and spending all their time with them, and all of a sudden, their friends and family fall to the bottom of the list—right down there with self-care.

I've been on the cover of many magazines and publications; I've been on television and have had a tremendous amount of success. People have celebrated how much money I've made, where I went to school, or how I built my company. But you never get accolades for being empathetic, sympathetic, forgiving, or practicing grat-itude. Our society is obsessed with the hustle and grind and the seeming "overnight success" that comes with building an empire. I thought *that* was feeding my soul, but it really wasn't. It was only making that empty place in my soul grow that much bigger and my need for relationships that much stronger. In reality, the things you get the least amount of recognition for are often the most important things in life.

Whether you have a new business, baby, job, relationship, or illness, it's important to take the time to catch up with your sister friends. Remember to tell them how much you love and appreciate them and how much you care. Let them be the shoulder you cry on when life's difficult moments hit, and remember to always be there for them in return. Text them just because and call them out of the blue. Just remember that maintaining real long-lasting relationships takes time and effort.

MORE THAN A TEAM

Cancer showed me, in more ways than one, that family goes far beyond the people who are related to us by blood. Family is also about those who are there for us when we need them the most. For me, this story wouldn't be complete without mentioning my employees.

My team at tgin stepped up in a major way and ran the company while I was out of commission. I never explicitly told them that I had breast cancer until long after the fact, but they knew something was up. When I first learned of my condition, my assistant had access to my emails, and our social media coordinator could see me liking and commenting on pictures that were breast-cancer related, so they were able to put two and two together. There was never a real discussion or meeting around my health, though; I just fell off the map. I would answer emails when I could, and they assured me that they were there for me no matter what I was going through. Multiple people sent me emails saying, "I don't know what's going on with you or why you haven't been here, but I'm praying for you. If you need anything, let me know."

The explosive success of the company wouldn't have been possible without these individuals holding tgin down for me while I was out. While I was worried about not having someone to lead this company that I'd built in the event that something happened to me, I realized the people who worked there believed it was their baby just as much as it was mine. I could tell by the emails coming in and out that everything was handled, and not having to worry took a lot of stress off of me. Orders were being shipped, nothing was late to Target, and customers were still happy. Since we were such a small team, we ultimately made the decision to pull back on events and marketing efforts and focus solely on making sure the day-to-day business responsibilities ran smoothly.

In business and life, who you surround yourself with

means everything. Some people call it finding your tribe. I learned that this is especially true when it comes to running a company. As an entrepreneur, your employees can mean the difference between getting to the next level and burning out. Now that I'm a more seasoned businesswoman, if I find myself working too hard, I realize that I have either a people or a process problem. If you don't have the right people on your team, business, or in your personal life, not only can you not beat cancer, but you can't take your company to the next level.

I've learned over the years that when it comes to growing and scaling a company, people are your best investment. I mean that in all seriousness. Having the right people in the right seats in your organization makes all the difference. People are better investments than billboards, samples, or any other marketing campaign. You by far earn the highest return on those who are not only super smart and hard-working, but those individuals who are invested in your mission, are passionate about what you do, and treat your company like it's their own. I wouldn't be where I am today, health- or business-wise, without the amazing team of people that I have surrounded myself with. With their help, diligence, loyalty, and unwavering commitment, they allowed me to come back bigger, better, and stronger than ever.

It's taken me forty years to realize that relationships are

the key to true richness and wealth. Who we have in our lives not only reflects what we value, but it shapes the people we become and impacts us in all aspects of life, whether personally, professionally, or spiritually. So, my grandmother may have been right after all. Family is everything. But I would make one modification, as we lawyers often do, to say, "Family is not just who we are related to by blood, but it's also our friends and loved ones…And they mean everything."

Chapter Twelve

---

25 MPH

Signing up for nine months of cancer treatments meant I had no choice but to slow down and put my health first.

Like most women, I've always felt overwhelmed. It seemed like the more I worked, the more work I had to do. I was literally drowning and struggling to stay afloat. But who doesn't feel that way? There were always emails to answer, phone calls to return, projects that needed to be completed, products that needed to be tested, and invoices that needed to be reviewed. I felt like if I took time to focus on myself, I would only fall further behind.

This was especially true before I found out I had cancer. Given my background as a lawyer, I always felt like things had to be perfect or damn near it, or there would be some kind of catastrophe. It was the way I had been trained professionally. I couldn't seem to help it.

For so long, I didn't have the ability to step back. Let me rephrase that. I didn't give myself permission to step back. I was constantly working, constantly on a treadmill. In my twenties and thirties, I was merely going through life crossing things off my list—things that I thought I was supposed to be doing versus the things I actually enjoyed doing.

When I received my diagnosis, I went home, got my affairs in order, cleaned up my house, organized my home office, threw a lot of stuff away, and focused on my health. I didn't know if this was the end, but in hindsight, I had to be prepared for the worst. Miraculously, during the time when I was sick and did the least amount of work, the company grew the most.

All of those fears I had about slowing down were ill-founded. All that pressure and anxiety that I'd carried with me for so long was for naught. My diagnosis was a powerful reminder that sometimes you have to slow down to speed up. Cancer ultimately taught me that you can't operate at 80, 90, or 100 mph all the time. You literally have to slow down, reduce your speed to 25, and in some cases, pull over to the side of the road, unpack your picnic basket, sit on the grass, and have a glass of Prosecco, or else you'll burn out.

Part of slowing down and taking better care of myself has meant letting go of the idea that I could have it all and do it all. As women, we must contend with images daily that suggest we're superhuman. We often have to take care of our families, keep our bodies tight, win in corporate America, get a masters, an MBA, a PhD, and do all of this with children on our hip. We have to be good moms, make the kids' lunches, get them to school, pick them up at the end of the day, take them to practice, keep their clothes clean, teach them to behave, and still get dinner on the table, and still find a way to do backflips in the bedroom. The list goes on for miles. Yet, no one stops to remind us that we have to put our oxygen mask on first before assisting others. We're often running on fumes, yet this is the very image of womanhood we're held to.

Even more, we live in a society where we feel an immense amount of pressure to be contoured to the gods, take a selfie with perfect lighting, and post about our amazing lives, our perfect children, and our accomplished selves. We have been conditioned to focus on gaining followers and counting likes, all the while making sure that no one sees our tears or knows how empty and alone this wall of technology makes us feel. Think about it. We live in a world that celebrates the idea of the hustle, the grind, and no sleep. What about celebrating slowing down? What if we were to highlight the women who invest in themselves, who take a step back, who practice self-care, who take off their capes and say, "I'm goalless as fuck, and I'm just going to focus on me."

As I continue to build tgin and its reach, I have to ask myself if I'm taking on a particular project because I want to make more money and have more notoriety or because it's something I actually enjoy and am passionate about. I also have to be more mindful about not having too many balls in the air. Before, I would work on a million important things at once and chase more money, but now, I have to pick and choose what is most important to me, prioritize, and focus my energy there. When I prioritize my life, I like to list out what's important to me and in what order. I've come to learn that if you don't set your priorities, someone else will.

Even as I give consideration to starting a second company or doing a book tour for this book, I've realized that I'm at a point in life where I need to shift my priorities. Everything is a tradeoff. When it comes to spending more time in the business, I have to ask myself if taking on more work would prevent me from getting married and starting a family. What would new projects mean for my self-care? I need to be conscious of these things, as I have not given them the proper consideration in the past.

Most recently, I've wanted to start a podcast, write this book, launch a new venture, and build my personal brand, which includes a blog and a website. I ultimately made the decision to put the podcast, website, and blog on the back burner if I was going to make time for myself and focus on my personal life. It was a first, and it was also hard because, at times, I see so many people on social media making so many power moves. The truth is, we should stop measuring our value based on how busy we are. Instead, we should celebrate how much time we spend with our families, how loyal we are to our friends, and how much joy our hobbies have given us. Again, I have to remind myself that less is more, and that I have to make myself a priority. When it comes to life and increasing your productivity, focusing on getting the right things done is key. Sometimes, we can accomplish this by investing in fewer activities, which allows us to make significant progress on the things that matter most. In my case, that's working towards starting and building my family.

Cancer has helped me to see that I was not putting the most important things first—my loved ones. Now, I'm working every day to change that by taking on less, saying no more, and making sure my personal goals get as much attention as my professional ones.

I'm learning, as a businesswoman, that doing less, and in some cases, absolutely nothing, is a great way to spend time. It's also a way to listen to your emotions and truly process what your body is sensing and feeling, which if left untreated, can manifest itself in other ways, like sickness and illness. In fact, I've learned that several major CEOs make it a point to block space off on their calendar to do nothing. Adopting this kind of approach can become a point of personal growth, enhancing both self-awareness and self-care.

This is also why I have recently taken up meditation. I previously thought mediating was something New Age that I just couldn't get into. At one time, sitting still and being quiet for longer than five minutes felt like torture. But now, I've grown accustomed to listening to nature sounds while lying in the bed every morning and then again in the late afternoon to help quiet my nerves and calm me. Meditation has come in handy when running into problems in the business because there are always fires to put out. Being a CEO is stressful. Being a woman CEO of a beauty company is even more stressful because of everything that comes along with having to look good all the time. Despite the fact that we have been doing this for years, we still run out of bottles, come close to missing deadlines, and sometimes, I have to let people go in the middle of our busiest season. Meditating allows me to center myself and minimize our problems, instead of treating them like catastrophes.

Research has shown that meditation helps with lowering the amount of stress hormones in our bodies, which increases our immunity against diseases, like cancer. This is probably the biggest reason why I've committed to this practice. I've seen the impact it has had on both my personal and professional life, and the results are amazing. I'm calmer and more in tune with my body, I have less stress because I remove whatever is stressing me from my life, and I'm more focused because I choose to live in the now. I still haven't mastered not checking my phone in the morning when I wake up, but it's a journey, and I'm happy with the progress I have made thus far.

So, I encourage you to set aside time to rest, to think, and to dream. Enjoy the moments of quiet and solitude that you create, and don't feel like you'll fall behind or fall apart if you take these small moments for yourself. Even if you do, it's sometimes for the better. Get out from underneath your emails. Take a walk. Call a friend. Create something, or just be strategic about your unscheduled moments. Slow down and take the time to focus on what matters most—you. Give yourself time, space, a clear head, and maybe a trip to the *Bali within* to pinpoint what you really value. It's a journey. It requires work and discipline, which means putting yourself first, but I promise you it's worth it.

Just remember, it's okay to sometimes take off your cape. In fact, I want you to.

Chapter Thirteen

COUNT YOUR BLESSINGS

When I was diagnosed with cancer, my first reaction was: "This is so unfair." After spending years devoting myself to building a company and helping other people, I was being dealt a major blow. At the time of my diagnosis, I felt as if I was at the prime of my life, both personally and professionally, but God dealt me this hand.

In the back of my mind, I wondered about the timing of it all. *Why me? Why now?* I considered myself to be a faithful Christian. I'm not saying I'm perfect; I'm definitely no angel, but I felt like my regular church attendance and strong relationship with God would keep me from going through something as trying as this. But there I was— young, single, and childless, with breast cancer and a super-fast-growing business, dealing with this unfortunate situation. For a minute there, I felt bad for myself, and I was also very angry with God. Along the journey, though, I gained perspective. I realized that if I was ever going to make it, I had to be grateful for everything that I had and who I was, instead of focusing on what I was lacking or who I wasn't.

For the first few weeks after receiving my diagnosis, I viewed myself purely as a cancer patient. I was Chris-Tia "Cancer" Donaldson. So much of this time was spent dealing with doctor's visits, testing, appointments, and letting people know how I was doing. It was like there was nothing more to talk about other than my disease. It was who I was, and I didn't feel like there was much more to me. However, as I progressed through my treatment, and particularly after scoring that big win at Target, I was able to realize that there was so much more to me than cancer and that I had a ton to be grateful for.

For me, the most challenging part about cancer treatment was the very beginning; extensive rounds of testing and the unforgiving hours spent waiting for the results were enough to drive me insane. When you go to a top research hospital like Northwestern, they are super cautious and take nothing for granted when it comes to X-rays or an MRI. It was like a never-ending rabbit hole of testing. I would go in for one round of tests and be cleared, but then the doctor would see something else, and in the interest of being cautious, they would order another round of tests.

Each time I went in for testing, I was scared as hell. If a test came back good, I felt like I dodged a bullet, but if something came back bad or uncertain, it was up in the air about whether they found more cancer or whether it spread to another part of the body. Stressful is an understatement. After dealing with all of the tests, multiple doctors, getting undressed and sitting on a cold exam table two to three times a week, and having fifty-plus people grab, squeeze, poke, and pull my boob, I started to develop a mild form of PTSD to the point that some doctors were even willing to prescribe me Xanax and other kinds of drugs to help me deal with the anxiety that came with this kind of treatment. It was truly traumatic, and once I got out of that testing phase, things started to turn a corner, and my treatment began to proceed fairly smoothly.

During chemotherapy, it was extremely common for me to have some nausea or loss of appetite. The best way to describe chemo is like a combination of early-pregnancy morning sickness and the aftermath of a night of endless Patrón shots. After a round of treatment, I often felt like I was hungover for four to five days, and then out of nowhere, I would start to slowly get better. Still, I became progressively tired. It was like no matter how much I slept, I was still tired.

After two or three rounds of chemo, I started to develop a routine to deal with the nausea and the metallic taste in my mouth—another common side effect of many cancer medications. As time went on, I came to appreciate the times I was up and able to move about, just as much as I had to appreciate the times when I was down on the couch for days. There would be days when I was strong and healthy, then there were days when I'd be so weak that I could barely get off the couch to take care of basic things around the house. The little moments when I could work out, eat, cook dinner, meet a friend, or just take a shower gave me so much joy. When I wasn't sick and laying on my couch, I wanted nothing more than to go out and spend time with friends or listen to music. When I saw an opportunity to enjoy life in between treatments, I knew I had to take it.

I still remember the night Prince died. April 21, 2016. I was on the up, and a guy from one of my business associations offered to take me home after a fundraiser. That night, he gave me his number and told me to text him but had no idea at the time that I was undergoing treatment. We ended up going to a Prince tribute that weekend and stayed out partying and drinking champagne until 2 a.m. while listening to the DJ play "Take Me with U."

We ended up dating for some time after that. I could go on, but little moments like that helped me to realize that even with cancer, I still had life left in me and people only saw what I projected.

After completing all eight rounds of chemo, I started to see light at the end of the tunnel and finally felt like I was able to start putting this health challenge behind me. Although I was still somewhat weak and fatigued, finishing chemo meant I was somewhat on the path to finding my "new normal," which you hear so many cancer patients talk about.

Still, I wasn't ready to jump back into my old life.

Life takes on a whole new meaning when you're sick and then healthy again. We all have experienced minor episodes like this, even when it's with a cold or flu. When you're down with a sore throat and fever, you're completely miserable and at your worst. When you start to feel better, it's like you're finally able to live your best life. The same is true with cancer.

Whether you're dealing with this disease or are in remission, life just seems so much fuller when you realize that you have the choice between viewing life in terms of whether you're living or dying. For me, I realized "healthy" was a state of mind and living meant enjoying life in the present moment. Now that I'm on the other side, little things like breathing, waking up in the morning, listening to music, working, and talking on the phone with my dad seem to have a whole new meaning. At the end of the day, it all comes down to being grateful for what I have right now, even when I feel like I don't have that much to be grateful for.

One day in particular truly shone a light on my gratitude. It was a Sunday morning; June 13, 2016, to be exact. I was lying on my couch in the midst of recovering from a recent chemo treatment. When I turned on the television, every major news station was covering the story of a twenty-nine-year-old security guard who had killed forty-nine people and wounded fifty-three others in a terrorist attack inside Pulse, a gay nightclub in Orlando, Florida. The stories and survivor tales were heart-wrenching. As individuals recounted their stories one after another for nearly forty-eight hours on every major news network, I sat wondering how they were gone and I was still here. I was at a major loss emotionally, but I could not fully grasp how all of those people innocently went out one night thinking they were going to have a good time, never to return home again. Just like that.

That was a pivotal moment in my cancer journey. I had to make a choice. Was I living or dying? It's a choice we all get to make every single day, even if it's not a completely active thought. That night, forty-nine innocent individuals went out to party and expected to come home to their loved ones, but they never did. Here I was on my couch battling cancer but still alive. No matter how you slice it, you have no idea how this game is going to end or where your chips are going to land. It was a huge eye-opener for me.

After seeing all the news reports and reading the interviews about the tragedy and loss that befell the families and friends of those victims, I kept thinking, "I'm still here. I'm still here. I'm still here." I made up my mind then and there to live each day to the fullest, no matter whether I was sick or in good health, no matter whether I was rich or poor, CEO or back working for someone else again.

Being grateful and giving thanks is much easier said than done, particularly in this day and age where we're constantly bombarded with images on social media of people living seemingly perfect lives. Even I find myself feeling slightly insecure when I grab my phone in the morning and this is the first thing that I see on my feed on Instagram. The 'gram can often make us feel like we're not enough, we're not accomplishing enough, or we don't have enough—or maybe even some combination of all three.

From the outside looking in, it appeared as though I was

doing well. I was an entrepreneur, running a "beauty empire," living this fabulous life, meeting with Target, closing deals, and making money. Not to mention, I looked like I was in great shape since I was down fifteen pounds, and my makeup, while natural, was on point. It was all so perfect. Very few people knew that I was battling a very serious illness or that my life was hanging in the balance. I managed to create a carefully curated image of what I wanted people to think my life looked like. This was more so for business than personal. It wouldn't have looked good to retailers and partners if I was completely MIA, so I had to give them something. While it appeared as though I had it all, nothing could have been further from the truth.

So many people, whether they'd admit it or not, are doing the same thing. It may not be cancer. It could be anything—struggling to keep up with debt, getting fired from their job, running a business with no customers, or pretending to be in the perfect marriage when they barely speak to their spouse. From the outside looking in, what we see on social media looks real, but a lot of it is smoke and mirrors.

Even to this day, as the owner of a beauty company, I feel some pressure to do this. We're all guilty of playing this game, and I own it. On more than one occasion, I've felt the need to cozy up to some of my good-looking, successful male friends to give people the impression that we're dating when nothing could be further from the truth. But like they say, we're not in the beauty business, we're in show business, because we're doing just that—putting on a show.

Still, I try to present an authentic reality as much as possible, even going so far as to show my bad hair days and tell the truth about entrepreneurship. Out of respect for my friends and loved ones, and to preserve a degree of inner peace, I have to maintain a certain degree of privacy. I just want to be honest and upfront and let people know that they're definitely only seeing part of this highly-photoshopped picture. No one sees the cancer, the failed relationships, the breakups, the friendships gone awry, the times I have had to dip into my personal savings to pay bills because the company was burning through cash, or the lonely nights on the couch. And with most people, they are giving you much less of the truth.

The truth is, we never know what's truly going on in people's lives. If we seek to empower ourselves and live our best lives, we have to be willing to find gratitude in our own situation.

Chapter Fourteen

MY PROMISE

I never wanted to be the "cancer girl." My friends, the few that I had, said there was some reason God chose me to endure this experience. While I have the belief that everything happens for a reason, I had a lot of emotions to deal with on the other side of cancer. Deep down inside, I knew I had to get myself right first.

Trust me, it's still an ongoing process. You never feel entirely right after going through something like this. But again, I had to find not only gratitude in being diagnosed with cancer but my purpose. I could have made the decision to live life broken and torn up, but instead, I found a way to pick myself up, put myself back together, live with my scars, and help those who were going through the same or similar situations. With women under forty only accounting for less than 5 percent of breast cancer diagnoses, it became vitally important for me to be an advocate and confidant for those undertaking this lonely journey.

I'm so eternally grateful that I made it and am able to be here today to speak about it. Unfortunately, a lot of women, particularly poor, black women, are not. What really stuck with me, though, was that I was treated at one of the top hospitals in the nation, if not the world. Without that care, or without my financial resources, I probably wouldn't be sitting where I am today, back in the saddle, living life, and traveling the world. Many women aren't here with us today simply because they didn't have the financial resources, education, or insurance that would have made all the difference.

After that eye-opening day in the South Side hospital waiting room, I remembered thinking to myself that if I ever got better, I would never forget about the uninsured and underinsured women who could not afford to go to Northwestern and receive the world-class medical treatment that I was fortunate to receive. I made a promise to myself that if I survived, I would become a voice for the voiceless.

People often think cancer + cancer treatment = cancer survivor. If only things were that simple. The road to survivorship is not a linear journey, and there are a lot of things along the way that can make a difference. I only realized this once I was on the other side. I also realized that my experience is highly unique in that I was diagnosed at one hospital and treated at another with vastly different resources and patient populations.

When it comes to cancer, money matters a lot. Very few people, including doctors, realize how much finances can become a barrier to proper treatment. I often tell people that I had the good fortune of reliable transportation, as well as the ability to pay eleven dollars each day for parking or the round-trip Uber fare to go to the hospital one hundred times in a single year. That's just $1,100 getting back and forth to the hospital, which is not covered by your insurance. For a lot of women, reliable transportation, gas money, a long ride, or an unpredictable bus schedule might be a barrier to treatment.

When I was going through cancer treatment, I was also single and childless, which was something I loathed, but came to find out, for many women, having reliable childcare while in treatment and during recovery may also be a barrier to survivorship. Patients under treatment don't have the luxury of just showing up when they want to. They're on a very specific schedule and have to be at the hospital during a very specific window because a cocktail or targeted therapy has been customized for their particular type of cancer. If they miss the bus or their boyfriend or husband needed to use their car, then they're shit out of luck.

I also tell people that I had the luxury of taking a 100 percent paid leave of absence due to my generous benefits at Oracle. To top it off, my boss was a breast cancer survivor, and my boss's boss gave me permission to take as much time off as I needed to get better. They literally assured me that my job would be waiting for me when I came back, and that my work load and assignments would be handled. I would not be sitting here today running this company and helping women dealing with this same condition if it were not for the generosity and support of my team at Oracle. During my time off, I could focus almost entirely on my health without any distractions, whereas many women are forced to choose. They have a limited number of days for taking time off or a jerk for a boss.

All of these things settled with me, and I realized that my experience was unique. When I share these stories with people, including doctors, many people are shocked to know that these kinds of basic financial issues can impact survivor outcomes.

In addition to the socioeconomic factors, a lot of systemic barriers contribute to the healthcare disparity that we see. When it comes to cancer treatment, for instance, safety net hospitals may not necessarily have fellowship-trained breast radiologists. They just have doctors who are trained to read X-rays and MRIs, and look for everything from breast cancer to broken bones to torn ligaments to slipped discs.

At a prominent hospital like Northwestern, radiologists are fellowship trained and board certified, meaning they have spent several years studying under a respected doctor on top of medical school to solely focus on breast cancer. When you see a top doctor with this kind of training, they're much more adept at picking up on cancers at an earlier stage because that's pretty much all they do. Top hospitals also have better equipment, better technology, and better policies, procedures, and practices for following up with patients after suspicious-looking images show up.

Research shows that poverty has a negative impact on the behavior of healthcare providers and the availability of health services. Healthcare practitioners who service minorities and people in low-income areas, for example, are often less informed about preventive care services and may not suggest screening tests, such as mammography.[2] Beth A. Jones, M.D., associate professor in the Department of Epidemiology and Public Health at Yale

---

[2] Gerend, Mary A. and Manacy Pai, *"Social Determinants of Black-White Disparities in Breast Cancer Mortality: A Review"* American Association of Cancer Research, January 26, 2019 http://cebp.aacrjournals.org/content/cebp/17/11/2913.full.pdf.

School of Medicine, led the study that says black women are almost twice as likely to report never receiving their mammography results and/or to report results that differed from those reported in the medical record as the general population. All of these factors play a role when it comes to breast cancer mortality rates amongst black women.

Fighting cancer was like being in a war. You were always seeing people go down to the left and right of you. Some would come home with purple hearts and others in body bags covered with the American flag. It was enough to deal with cancer itself, but on your tour of duty, you saw people who didn't make it. Not only do you have to deal with your own fears, pain, and panic, but you also deal with survivor's guilt. It's a sad reality to think you were fortunate enough to continue living and other people were not. Just like with the Orlando shooting.

Sitting in that waiting room on the south side of Chicago, I was surrounded by so much hopelessness. But I made a promise to myself that I would always tell the story of the strong women battling alongside me, so other people who came after us could feel like this is a condition worth fighting through—that their life is worth fighting for—and that breast cancer doesn't have to be a death sentence. This book helps fulfill my promise.

Despite the regrettable and discouraging health dispar-ities, the truth is African-American women aren't dying from breast cancer largely due to biological reasons. Although black women are more likely to have triple negative cancer, meaning the cancer is not hormonally sensitive and therefore more difficult to treat, socioeco-nomic factors play a major part in why black women are not beating this disease. We know this because in cities like Chicago, black women are 42 percent more likely to die from breast cancer than their white counterparts; but in cities like New York City, that number drops to 19 per-cent. In San Francisco, it drops to 0 percent, largely due to programs that offer affordable access to healthcare.[3]

In the past, black women were less likely to get breast cancer but more likely to die from it. Now they're as likely to get breast cancer as white women and still more likely to die from it.

WE'RE WORKING TO FIX THIS. YOU CAN TOO.

As a result of my experience, my team and I have decided that one of our key priorities for tgin's philanthropy would be breast cancer education and awareness, particularly

---

3   Hunt, Bijour R, Steve Whitman, and Marc S. Hurlbert. *"Increasing Black:White disparities in breast cancer mortality in the 50 largest cities in the United States"*, The International Journal of Cancer Epidemiology, Detection, and Prevention, January 26, 2019, https://www.sciencedirect.com/science/article/pii/S1877782116301114

with respect to how this condition impacts African-American women and women under the age of forty.

When I finally revealed my diagnosis on social media, the outpouring of support was unbelievable. We learned that many of our customers had a mother, sister, aunt, grandmother, best friend, or teacher that was impacted by this disease. We also encountered several men who were also afflicted with this condition. Many people, myself included, were surprised to learn of its impact on the opposite sex.

While I thought I was young when I was diagnosed at thirty-six, along this journey I have met women who were diagnosed with breast cancer as young as twenty-two. They weren't just anomalies, because there are definitely many more; we just haven't heard their stories. As a result, we, at tgin, have used our platform to shed a light on these individuals, so young women don't mistakenly believe that they are immune to this disease just because the recommended age for starting mammograms is forty.

We, at tgin, hope to eliminate the health disparities facing our community by raising awareness and staying active in the cause. Our mission-based passion project has allowed me to combine my interest in being a voice with my passion for being a businesswoman, which ultimately led to the creation of the tgin Foundation. Although our not-for-profit organization is still fairly young and new, with time, we hope to continue to have a considerable impact on the community and be a new voice in the conversation around how breast cancer impacts women of color.

Chapter Fifteen

TRUE LOVE

I travel all over the country speaking at schools, universities, meet-ups, book clubs, coffee shops, art galleries, business conferences, you name it. I get asked about almost everything, but the one thing most women are curious about, but are often too scared to ask, is my love life. There have been numerous instances where I've been in a room full of women, and they'll ask everything imaginable about building a company and starting a business. *Why did you leave your job? How did you juggle the company and battle cancer? What's next for you? Do you regret going to law school? How have you seen yourself professionally over the years?* But behind all this ambition and drive, the one burning question I know they are too scared to ask is, *How is your love life?*

They might be scared to put me on the spot in front of

an entire audience, or they might not want to pry, but on more than one occasion, a few brave women have pulled me aside and said, "I don't want to be too personal, but what is it like dating as a CEO?" or "What is it like being single and successful?" Some of us are so ambitious and driven in our careers that we're completely lost or unfocused when it comes to our personal relationships, and that applies to both the people we date and the people we befriend. So, I applaud the women who have been bold enough to ask how I juggle my professional drive with my desire to find love and partnership. I'm baring it all here, so no judgment, please.

I think my concept of love is somewhat skewed. I grew up in what many would have considered to be a functional household. My parents were actually in love. They weren't just performing for friends, family, or followers; this was way before public anniversary messages, ring shots, thank you for the flowers, and subliminal messages on Facebook. Their love was genuine; you could just look at them and tell. It was that simple. Although my dad wasn't the most affectionate person during my childhood, I grew up with a very powerful example of what true love looked like, and I wanted it for myself.

My parents traveled all over the world. They'd ditch us kids and go on dates every Saturday night. They embraced "his" and "her" roles when it came to housework and chores, and for the most part, they maintained a united front whenever my sister or I gave them trouble. When my mom was featured in the newspapers or honored with an award, my dad was proud, and it showed, and vice versa. I will never forget falling asleep in the back seat of their car in my pajamas as Anita Baker and the Isley Brothers played on the radio after they'd pick me up from my grandma's house after a romantic evening. Nearly twenty-two years after my mother died, it's clear to me and everyone else, including the women he has dated since losing her, that my dad is still very much in love with my mom.

Back then, most of what I experienced was through the eyes of a child. In many ways, this became problematic and part of the reason why I was single for so long. I viewed true love between two equally successful partners as something achievable that I wanted for myself. Yes, I've put up with dysfunction in my relationships, but those were the relationships that also had no chance of becoming lifetime commitments.

I longed for commitment, but I often rejected relationships that didn't meet my expectation of what being in love should look like. Growing up, I wasn't exposed to a great deal of conflict, nor did I witness any kind of abuse, be it physical, mental, verbal, or emotional, so my long-term tolerance for this kind of behavior has always been low.

Although both of my parents were extremely successful and did well for themselves, I never saw my father openly compete with my mother or try to undermine her, like so many men I have dated. Still, no marriage is perfect, but sadly, my mom wasn't around long enough to tell me how hard marriage is and what love truly entails. With such a powerful example of black love growing up, I was unwilling to settle for something that was less than that. It became hard to commit to a relationship and devote myself to a man who was unable to show me the same kind of love that my dad expressed towards my mother. My parents ultimately set a very high standard for me for how I, as a black woman, should be treated, and many of my relationships could never live up to that.

On top of that, as a kid, I grew up watching shows like *The Cosby Show* and *A Different World*, which highlighted very positive examples of black love. I thought I would go to Hillman College and easily meet my Dwayne Wayne—someone smart, a little nerdy, but cute. In my childhood fantasies, we'd fall in love, get married when I was twenty-five, have kids when I was twenty-eight, and live happily ever after. There were so many examples back then in film, television, and music, almost too many to name. Denise Huxtable went away and married a hot soldier. Eddie Murphy fell in love with Halle Berry in the movie *Boomerang*. And, at least on camera, Martin and Gina seemed to be smitten with one another.

Back then, movies like *Love Jones* and *Love and Basketball* made love seem so easy, achievable, and to some degree, drama-free.

Before cancer, I was driven by two things: money and men. When I look back on the years I spent dating, I've been in relationships that felt like a constant replay of the same movie. I was starring in my own version of *Fast and Furious 9*. I had a boyfriend here and there, but for the most part, my interactions with men were more akin to situation-ships than relationships.

In my mid-twenties and well into my thirties, I often chose emotionally unavailable men who were not really looking for much other than a good time. We would always start off on the good foot, hang out, kick it, talk every day. We'd have drinks and dinner, exchange text messages, and spend late nights together on repeat for nine months to a year and a half until something would pop off, and I'd say I was done. I was never one of those "where is this going" kind of chicks, which may have given it away from the beginning that I wasn't exactly looking for something long-term and stable.

I also didn't really have a physical type. Some were tall; others were taller; most were professional. All of them were funny and smart, but most of them left me crying, frustrated, and wanting more. Maybe it was another girl, their career, their finances, their ego, or their drinking, but I felt at the time like there was always something that prevented us from taking things to the next level.

I've dated rich guys, poor guys, nine-to-five guys, CEOs, construction workers, and everything in between. I found myself choosing between men my own age who were professionally trying to "figure themselves out," who were intimidated by my success, and *unwilling* to commit, and older, successful men who showered me with attention, helped me navigate my personal and professional life, and who were *unable* to commit.

Neither situation was truly ideal, but given my ambition and accomplishments, what's a single, thirty-something-year-old girl to do? When it came to love, I often felt like I had a better chance of getting struck by lightning or winning the lottery than finding the one.

I realize now that my failed relationships had more to do with my choices than the men I was dating. They say your relationship with your mate is a reflection of your relationship with yourself. Looking back on my life, I kept choosing emotionally unavailable men because I was emotionally unavailable myself. There were many breakups, but there would always be someone waiting in the wings. My motto was always "on to the next." Just as in law, when it came to love, I always had a plan B and found myself often dating, or at least entertaining, more than one guy at a time. Back then, I treated dating like an investment; I definitely wanted to diversify. Even if I was really into a guy, I was never willing to go all in and put all my chips on one stock. What if the market crashed, and I got hurt and was left penniless without anyone to move on to?

It wasn't until I got cancer and started to unpack the things that hurt me, the traumas I experienced, the heartbreaks I felt—all of which had nothing to do with men—that I started to make progress in the emotionally-available department. Writing this book and putting my thoughts, fears, and pain on paper have been a critical part of this process.

I didn't have time to fully invest in relationships, because I could barely make the time to invest in myself. I lied to myself and said I wanted a commitment because it sounded nice, but I'm not sure if I was truly ready at the time for what it meant to be in a partnership, even though I did a good job of pretending that I did.

So many times, I found myself trying to be something I wasn't, in order to make a man feel better about himself, because I never believed anyone could love me for the smart, beautiful, driven, sassy woman that I am. I don't have to be the smartest person in the relationship, but I can't count the number of times where I have withheld an opinion or refrained from saying something for fear of trouncing on someone's ego. I can't even count how many times I have allowed myself to engage in relationships with people who pretended to be there for me and for us when they really weren't. Some men say they're attracted to a woman's ambition, drive, passion, or intelligence, but everything in their actions suggests otherwise. They date other women while they're in a relationship with us, or they attack how often we work or the job we're doing. Without my mother to guide me, I was left to my own devices and had to rely on my girlfriends, many of whom were in similar situations, to navigate the dating landscape. The truth is, I should have been true to myself, even if it meant it limited my dating pool.

A lot of this was inertia, and a lot of it was being so busy with the company that I didn't have the time to stop and reflect on my choices. Although I was in therapy on and off for years, I was not breaking any kind of cycle. Looking back on it, I can see why. I never wanted to talk about my mom, and as a result, I couldn't really get to the root of my decisions. Really, it all came down to this simple fact: I never wanted to get so close to someone and love them in that way, only for them to leave me again. #breakthrough

SUPERMAN

But, there's always one. You know the one; where enough is enough. He's the one that solidifies that you'll never put up with another man's shit. He's the baggage you bring into every relationship. For me, that was Superman. We started dating in 2013, when tgin was literally just getting off the ground. He knew I was a lawyer and thought it was "cute" that I had a hair care company on the side.

When we first met, our relationship was amazing. He was super supportive and super into me. I was smitten with the fact that he was always rooting for the company. He would straighten up my shelf in Mariano's, and even told me, *"One day, you're going to be in Target right next to Shea Moisture."* The thing is, he was just being nice. I honestly don't think he ever believed it would happen, but it sounded so good.

When we actually did launch in Target, he ghosted me.

He'd come in and out of my life like clockwork. Every August, he would show up just when construction season was over, and then, every April, he would completely disappear. It became almost laughable how predictable it was. He would start a fight about something small or just completely fall off the radar.

The first time it happened was in 2013, and I was crushed.

At the time, he often told me how he could see a life for us together, and that I was wife material. The relationship was going so well, and out of nowhere, he decided that he wanted "to focus on his job and raising his kids." I was completely crushed. Two weeks later, he was on Facebook with his arm around his ex-girlfriend at someone's birthday party. She was a fitness instructor, and running outside was their summer thing. Then that fall, he came back around with his tail between his legs, and we cooked and grilled, spent the holidays together, exchanged gifts, watched Netflix, and chilled until spring. Then, April of 2014 came around, and he disappeared again.

When he went back to his ex, I often found myself asking: *"Why her? What does she have that I don't? Is she better looking than me? Smarter than me? What is she that I'm not?"* One of the unhealthiest attributes of these bad relationships is when we start comparing ourselves to other women.

Over time, I adjusted my dating strategy and just started rotating other players off the bench to account for his comings and goings. But then, he showed up again in the fall of 2014 when I was working on the Target launch. During this time, he was extremely supportive and cheered for me from the sidelines, and I fell for it once again. But when my dream actually came to fruition and we landed on the shelves, he couldn't handle it. A week after our

Target launch party, he picked a fight with me and disappeared without a trace. He resurfaced some time later, but I reached a point where I wasn't putting up with it anymore. We decided to be friends, but I wasn't going to let him back into my life completely. This meant we could talk on the phone, but I refused to invite him over and be in his presence. I was tired of the crazy vicious cycle of on again, off again, and had finally reached a point where I was ready to move on.

But later that year, I got cancer. He initially wanted to come see me and was super supportive, but I told him I was good and that we could talk on the phone from time to time. Little by little, I let my guard down. He came to see me, he called me every day, he made all these romantic overtures. He even came over and shaved my head, rubbed my back, and called me after every chemo treatment in the very beginning, just to make sure I was okay. He would spend the night, hold me in his arms, and tell me how beautiful I was, all the while making plans for what we were going to do together once I recovered.

Then out of nowhere, April came, and he disappeared again. I looked up on Facebook, and this time there's a new girl, and they're dating. Wait, no, they're in love. Wait, no, they're buying a house. Wait, fuck, they're getting married. It all happened so fast. Hurt couldn't even begin to describe how I felt. I was fighting for my life, and the last thing I could do was be bothered with someone who had shown me time and time again who he was. I had no choice but to move on and focus on regaining my health. When I was wrapping up treatment, I barely thought about him. However, when I completely finished, the whole situation finally sunk in, and I was hurt that someone would take advantage of me while I was sick and on my back. Still, I must own my choices. I let him in.

Moral to the story: men don't ever just break up with a girl or disappear without having a place to go. They aren't risk takers in that sense. They always have something teed up and ready to go before they pull the little disappearing act that I've seen over and over. It's just a way to keep you hanging on the door in case they decide to come back. If you're in a similar situation and reading this, highlight the first sentence in this paragraph and put a giant star next to it. It will save you a lot of heartache, worry, and time spent on the phone with your girlfriends, wondering where he went. Ninety-nine percent of the time, it's another girl, not his sick dad, his busy schedule, or his kids. Mark my word.

So, as you can see, I was not only a great air traffic controller but an awesome paramedic, who had mastered the art of giving CPR to dead relationships. We can sometimes find ourselves in these toxic situations, holding onto things that were clearly dead a long time ago, because we've invested so much and are determined to make it work. Instead, we should just drop them and focus on loving ourselves.

On some level, love, or even stable relationships, eluded me for a very long time. Love is completely irrational; and given that I'm a logical person, it was sometimes hard for me to comprehend how I was supposed to trust another person. How could I let go and give myself completely to someone who could disappoint me over and over again? I'm used to dealing with things that I can touch and see. That's why I work with numbers. They always tell a story; things have to add up. As a logical being always trying to make sense of things, love is one of those things that just *is*. You can't see it or touch it. It's elusive. But you can feel it. Love doesn't always add up or make sense, but I have learned that you have to be willing to love unconditionally to experience love at its deepest levels. This can be extremely hard when you have twenty years of baggage to deal with, especially when you have failed to come to terms with the role you played in your own choices.

Breast cancer forever altered the course of my life and how I think about loving another person. After undergoing treatment, my eyes were open to my vulnerabilities as a person, with all my cracks and flaws. This journey humanized me. I wasn't robotic before, but my heart needed to be softened. I became more in touch with my emotions than I'd ever been in the past. Cancer helped me take off the mask and realize that I wanted to live life on my terms. When I was able to truly embrace that philosophy and live life unapologetically, I was able to find true love.

My thinking on love is completely different now. Prior to my diagnosis, I always had to have a plan. I always had to know what was coming next. I had to be days, weeks, or months ahead of the game. Whether it was product development, event planning, or budgeting, I had to be ready. That's what lawyers do. I often approached relationships the same way. A lot of times, I might have tried to control things or make sure everything was running on some kind of timeline instead of taking my hands off the wheel and letting things happen naturally.

Professionally, I wasn't conditioned to just let things happen, and I didn't see a lot of success when people did that. Up until then, I believed that you work for what you want, and what you put into a situation is what you get out of it. I thought that was true when it came to love. But when cancer came calling, I had to learn to let go in all aspects of life. When I did, the company did well. My relationships with my family members improved. Even my health got better. Realizing there was a pattern, I decided to adopt the same approach when it came to romantic relationships.

I also feel less pressured to find love and get married now, whereas before, like many women, I felt I needed to be with someone in order to feel validated. Over the years, despite all of my professional and personal accomplishments, I've always felt social pressure from my family to get married—some well-meaning and some just outright shade. There was a time when I approached family gatherings with somewhat of a pit in the bottom of my stomach. Although most of my family is totally cool, there is always that one aunt who constantly asks if I'm dating, when I'm getting married, and when I'm having kids. For many of us, these are things that are absolutely out of our control, but some people love to shine a light on what they believe you're lacking, to make themselves feel better.

Not only have we been conditioned from a young age to have these titles, but we're constant recipients of unsolicited opinions on who we should marry and by when. We're always under the microscope for our choices. That causes some of us to rush off into bad situations with the hope of eliminating that feeling of pressure, the biological clock combined with your family's expectations.

I found that, after my treatments, I was able to let go and ignore so many of those pressures. I was at a point where I didn't care whether I got married; I was just so grateful to be alive. I previously thought that being able to say I was married would bring me some kind of relief. I used to long to fall in love, get married, and have kids. Now, I realize that it doesn't have to happen in that order. I don't have to be married to have a baby, and I don't have to get married if I fall in love. I just have to be open to the possibilities and be grateful for what I have in that given moment. What matters most in life is being able to live on your own terms—not your mom's, dad's, aunt's, or Instagram's terms, but your terms. And that couldn't be any more true, especially when it comes to love.

My love life did change after cancer.

At first, a small part of me still felt like no one would ever want me again. My breast surgeon did an amazing job and left me with minimal signs of the lumpectomy, but I still have scars on my body that were not there before. In the past, I could hide whatever it was that I had been through. Now, my scar from my chemo port stares at me in the mirror every day and is super prominent when I wear a low-hanging top. It's a small price to pay but still something that takes getting used to.

Every time I take my clothes off, the physical signs of what I have been through are there. My right breast, where the cancer was found, is now concave and slightly smaller than the left. Things don't look exactly the way they were before, nor do they stand up as nicely. There's also additional medication I need to take for the next ten years, and on top of that, I have to deal with stress and weight gain. Coming back into the dating realm with all this physical, emotional, and mental baggage was a lot. I felt like damaged goods.

I'm very much emotionally scarred, as well, particularly with the concerns around my fertility and having to explain to someone that having kids probably won't be that easy, and we would definitely require some help. Having to deal with that and the fact that I had breast cancer, made me feel like my dating stock had dropped. I was now a person with a health issue, an illness. I always felt the pressure to check my baggage at the door when I came into any kind of relationship, and now, I don't have that option. Before, my baggage was that I was a workaholic, but I could hide that. Now, I'm a former cancer patient. I don't know how many guys would be looking to sign up for that.

However, a certain brokenness and vulnerability comes with scars, no hair, no eyebrows, and a concave boob. Those physical signs make me imperfect in my own eyes, and I think people are beginning to be even more attracted to that. It has become a counterbalance to my professional accomplishments. I now give off an energy that attracts people who are willing to be emotionally vulnerable and reveal their scars. I'm more carefree and less focused on a timeline. I can live in the moment, let go, and see where life takes me rather than always wondering where things are going.

The same way I had to let go and let my doctors and God take over is the same thing I have to do to find true love. There's something about that openness that allows me to attract different types of individuals, ones who are fine with me being an Alpha chick, but also kind and caring enough to want to be with someone who had previously been diagnosed with cancer.

True love is rare, and even harder to find. It is unconditional, the kind of love where the person really accepts you for more than your looks, more than your money, more than your physical attributes. They love you just as you are. I've learned that it takes a special kind of courage, a kind that I did not have before, to not only love someone for who they are, but to be willing to be vulnerable enough to be the recipient of that kind of love in return.

Chapter Sixteen

THE GREATEST LOVE OF ALL

As much as cancer taught me about loving someone else, it also revealed to me the importance of loving myself.

For the first time in my life, I truly understand why it is so important to love myself. It's so cliché, but I get it now. I used to be so hard on myself. I held myself to such an impossibly high standard. Being brought down to such a valley and then coming back with these scars forced me to be more forgiving and kind to myself. I learned to recognize that I was never going to be perfect. No situation was going to be perfect. And my imperfections and battle wounds were beauty marks more than anything.

The lesson here is that you've got to deeply love yourself

and all of your imperfections before expecting someone else to do the same. All along, I had been searching for someone who would be willing to love me and accept all my flaws and imperfections, but I was always striving to be perfect, to be excellent, and was unwilling to accept anything less. I had to get to the point of self-acceptance first, and truly understand that God loves me unconditionally, before someone else could come along and love me the way I needed them to. Once I changed my own standards and became more kind and loving to myself, I was able to attract more loving, kind relationships.

During this journey, I also realized the value of spending time by myself. As a society, we often think one of the worst things that can happen to you is dying alone. As a single woman, this fear had definitely crossed my mind several times, but during my treatments, this fear subsided.

A lot of people crave companionship. Beyond their fear of dying alone, they want the comfort of knowing that someone would care for them if something bad happened. Yet, I saw a lot of women going through this journey who were either married, going through a divorce, or single that, for one reason or another, thought someone would be there for them, and they weren't. Having a significant other doesn't necessarily mean that person will live up to your expectations or be there for you through your difficult moments.

The truth is, the human spirit is much more resilient than we think it is. Sometimes, it's better to be by yourself than in a relationship. You might find it's easier to move through these kinds of challenges without someone adding stress to your life or having someone around who isn't really in your corner.

Relationships are great, of course. There's nothing like a warm human being to embrace, to talk to, to listen to, and to love. We're all meant to have a loving counterpart. But even with the perfect guy—and there are none of those around—we still need spiritual nourishment.

Relationships are a beautiful thing, but what many won't admit is that you can be in a relationship and still feel the same kind of emptiness that you feel when you're single. I know I have in the past. Sometimes, it has something to do with your partner and what they may be lacking, and other times, it has absolutely nothing to do with that person that you're in a relationship with. That empty feeling that we're constantly looking to fill may be the space in life that is meant for a relationship with God. It can't be filled by money, a bigger house, a car, a boyfriend, or even a child. That empty little space in your chest can only be filled with the contentment and peace that comes with being present, letting go, and trusting in your relationship with God.

I often heard people say that cancer is a gift or blessing

from God. I never knew what they meant until the very end. Although it's a blow to your ego to be sick, and your days are spent sitting in doctor's appointments and laying on the couch eating apple sauce, for me, it was one of the most calming experiences of my life. It was during my battle with cancer that I had the closest relationship with God, with nothing coming in between us.

When you find yourself going through something difficult, and you start feeling like things will never be right again, those are the times when you often experience God's presence the most. These critical moments are when your relationship deepens and develops with the Divine. It's during these moments that we learn that we can truly count on God no matter what.

There were times when I was undergoing treatment where I was just too proud to admit that I was scared of being alone. I'm not sure if I was afraid that something was going to happen from a physical standpoint or if it was just the fear that I was no longer capable of defending myself in the way that I was used to. I soon came to realize that I was never alone. My dad would fly in for my appointments and my therapy sessions, but he wasn't by my side 24/7. There was a point when I started to turn a corner, when I still talked to him every day, but I didn't need to be looked after so closely. During those times, he may have been out with his friends or playing golf while I was lying on the couch resting. I'm still grateful for those moments of solitude because they truly showed me that I could be alone in a physical sense but would never be alone in the spiritual sense. Those moments also serve as powerful reminders that I have everything I need to face any challenge and overcome any obstacle.

* * *

The words of the poem, "Footprints in the Sand," have always rung true for me. It tells the story of a man who takes a walk on the beach with the Lord. At one point in the poem, the man realizes that during his lowest times, there's only one set of footprints in the sand. Of course, he gets upset by this, thinking that God has abandoned him at his worst, but it's revealed that, instead, those were the times the Lord carried him out of his darkness.

In your darkest times in life, God will be the one to carry you and help you make it through your struggles. My dad was there, my Uncle Willie was there, some of the guys I dated were here and there, but God was always there. In our darkest hours, it's important to remember to hold fast to God's unchanging hand and know that we're never alone. We're safe in God's love, strength, power, and wisdom.

My relationship with God, which I always thought was

strong, deepened during this time. Seeing what he was able to do for me, without my assistance, left me in awe of his powers. I gained a greater appreciation of my life, and the role he played in it.

In life, your faith will be tested. During these difficult moments, your faith, courage, and wisdom will be strengthened. You just have to trust the process. The journey is not perfect, nor is it linear, but life is beautiful—even in your darkest moments. It can be easy to want to give up or remain stuck in your old, damaging ways, but I think the purpose of any dark time in life is to show you that there's always a light at the end of the tunnel, to make you appreciate the gift of life that has been so gently placed upon you. Anything is possible when you have the love and support of God holding you up.

His message for me had always been clear, but my ego and pride wouldn't allow me to see it. His message for you is just as apparent. But are you going to give thanks for the many amazing things you have, or will it take something drastic to make you open your eyes and see the good that has been bestowed upon you? The choice is yours.

CONCLUSION

Every August since being diagnosed with cancer, I've made the trek to Bali. Instead of going there looking for peace, I now use the time away to reflect on who I was before, who I have become, and where I go from here. When the reader in Bali gave me the advice back in 2016 about finding the Bali within, I knew I had to do the work with a capital "W" in order to find my place of inner peace. Writing this book and coming to grips with my painful past have been a major part of that.

For the last year, I have had to sit with my feelings, something I don't ordinarily do, because I've been so conditioned, like many of us, to bury my pain and move on quickly. Strangely enough, because this book felt like real work, I actually committed to completing it. In turn, this process has been akin to therapy and my personal way of processing my emotions.

Over the course of this project, I found that many of the chapters were exceptionally painful to write. There were many times where I would be sitting at my computer crying as I described my relationship with my mom and what it felt like to miss her nearly twenty-two years after she'd passed, as well as how I learned of my diagnosis. The pain was so immense that I didn't have the strength to go back and edit them or reread them all over again. I had to rely on my team, in many instances, to clean up parts of this story as it was just too painful to relive. It is my hope that I, too, can one day read this book from cover to cover and appreciate my growth and how far I have come. I'm slowly getting better at acknowledging my pain instead of running from it. And for that, I'm proud of myself. #babysteps

I've had a chance to not only reflect on my life, my cancer diagnosis, the loss of my mom, my many failed relationships, my lack of work-life balance, and what kind of daughter, sister, and friend I have been, but this project has helped me to realize my God-given purpose. I now know that I have been blessed with the position of CEO, not so I can be some mega beauty mogul, but so I can ultimately shed light on the health disparities that plague uninsured and under-insured women afflicted with breast cancer. Now, only a few years after being diagnosed with this disease, the answers to "Why me? Why now?" are clearer than ever. It was all a test, as all of life is. But it was to prepare me for my journey and show me with complete clarity that I have work to do in this world.

Taking this trip back down memory lane has also helped me to realize the importance of being kind to myself and why sometimes we have to take off our cape and put all of that Superwoman nonsense aside. I've also come to grips with the fact that no one has it all. Whether it's love or business, I have to run my own race and live life on my own terms.

I am forever grateful for the opportunity to have documented my storm, and that you have taken this deeply personal journey with me. I now have a powerful reminder of the strength of God and the role He has played in my life. I have also made peace with the fact that no matter the storm, I have no choice but to trust that God will see me through difficult times.

I hope my testimony gives hope to those who are in the midst of a storm and to those who find themselves being prepared for one they'll face in the future, be it cancer or something else. Just know that you can go through a Category 5 hurricane and still stand tall. You may come out on the other side bruised, soaking wet, and broken, but you have to keep going—no matter what. Everything will be okay. What may seem difficult or insurmountable today will be a distant memory in time. It may be hard to accept when you're going through something challenging, but there is good and purpose in every difficult situation. Step back long enough to see your situation for what it is. Find your peace and hold fast to God's unchanging hand.

A storm is nothing more than a test. Just like the ones in nature, it doesn't last forever. Whether you pass or fail comes down to whether you choose to keep going. While no one will get through this life unscathed, what you learn from life's tests is what drives you to become a stronger person. Understand that your trials and tribulations make you who you are. So, stand with me in gratitude as we take on these tests with strength and diligence, for it's through these obstacles that we experience the true essence of what it means to live.

ACKNOWLEDGMENTS

I want to first thank God for giving me the strength to fight this battle, and for using this dark moment in my life to help me walk in my greater purpose and empower other women to listen to their bodies and put themselves first.

Mom, although you weren't here long, I want to thank you for being a remarkable example of womanhood and instilling in me a strong sense of confidence and the unshakable belief that I could accomplish anything.

Dad, what can I say? We've been on this journey for forty years together. You're my ride or die and have always had my back. I will always appreciate you for your wisdom and insight, and for being a strong role model when it comes to having faith and trusting in God. You always have the answers. No matter what, I know that I can always turn to you.

Uncle Willie. You're a gem. I wouldn't be where I am today if you had not moved to Chicago to watch my baby. You are crazy as a Betsy bug, but you're always right. If anyone has taught me how to slow down and know that everything is going to be alright, it's you. I'm so glad you came into my life.

Aris and Piper, thank you for packing up your entire life and moving from Houston to Chicago on a moment's notice when the enemy wanted to act up. Your constant prayers and belief in me have allowed me to take this company to the next level.

To all my employees, past and present, we made it. Kristin, thanks so much for holding down the fort and dealing with my scattered personality and over-the-top perfectionism for years. Kenesha, Sara, Maria, Irma, Ashley, Shelon, Brittany, and Bree, you will always be my day ones.

Stephanie, I am forever grateful to you for your honesty and perspective when it came to this project. You've been there from the very beginning, and it means so much. Taylor, Erica, Lyric, and Eric, thank you for your edits, feedback, and suggestions. We hit this one out the park!

To our customers, thank you for your support over the last ten years. It means the world to me. You are the reason why I do what I do.

Finally, to my team at Scribe, y'all killed it. I don't know if I would have made it to the finish line without you. Shout out to John for being all over me and reminding me every week that done is better than perfect. Robyn, you were incredible and did an awesome job of bringing my story to life. Mark, you laid a remarkable foundation, which allowed me to find my best voice.

To anyone that I may have missed, thank you!

ABOUT THE AUTHOR

CHRIS-TIA DONALDSON was once just a street-smart girl from Detroit with a passion for hair and a dream of owning her own business. Now a two-time Harvard University graduate, bestselling author, and lifestyle expert, she is also the founder and CEO of a nationally distributed beauty brand, Thank God It's Natural (tgin). Her products are sold in Target, Ulta, Sally Beauty Supply, Walgreen's, and Whole Foods, and the company continues to grow. Chris-Tia has been named one of Chicago's 40 Under 40 and has been featured in *USA Today*, *Marie Claire*, *Essence*, *Black Enterprise*, *Heart & Soul*, and the *Chicago Tribune*.